Heir of Narcissism

Exploring ADHD in the Context of Complex Trauma

Michael Drag, LPC

Copyright © 2025 by Michael Drag

All rights reserved.

No portion of this book may be reproduced in any form without written permission from the publisher or author, except as permitted by U.S. copyright law.

This publication is designed to provide accurate and authoritative information in regard to the subject matter covered. It is sold with the understanding that neither the author nor the publisher is engaged in rendering legal, investment, accounting or other professional services. While the publisher and author have used their best efforts in preparing this book, they make no representations or warranties with respect to the accuracy or completeness of the contents of this book and specifically disclaim any implied warranties of merchantability or fitness for a particular purpose. No warranty may be created or extended by sales representatives or written sales materials. The advice and strategies contained herein may not be suitable for your situation. You should consult with a professional when appropriate. Neither the publisher nor the author shall be liable for any loss of profit or any other commercial damages, including but not limited to special, incidental, consequential, personal, or other damages.

First paperback edition May 2025
ISBN (paperback) 978-1-967638-01-7

NO AI TRAINING: Without in any way limiting the author's exclusive rights under copyright, any use of this publication to "train" generative artificial intelligence (AI) technologies to generate text is expressly prohibited. The author reserves all rights to license uses of this work for generative AI training and development of machine learning language models.

No generative AI was used to create this book.

Book design by DragonPen Designs
Cover illustration by Selina J. Eckert

*To those who feel the world was not made for them:
Let's break the system together.*

An Open Letter to the Highly Critical Parent

    I want to write this letter to any parent who might choose to pick up this book or even be shown it by a loved one who is reaching out to save a relationship. People do not tend to abandon their loved ones easily, even if for a time it might be what is best for them. I implore anyone who reads this to do your very best to meet the needs being asked of you or to at least not respond with harm.
    Children idolize their parents, even when those children might have deserved a much gentler hand in guiding them. They did not choose to come into this world and suffer. Many have even chosen to leave this world instead of hurting those who have hurt them. As infants, we are encoded to understand our place in the world through the eyes that reflect us, our parents. A highly critical parent will lead to a highly self-critical child and, later, adult. They will be plagued with depression and anxiety. They will be successful at the cost of their mental health and relationships, or they may be unable to achieve anything if the weight is too much. It is not in their power to make this decision, as every decision they make is based on every experience they have had from the day they were born. The power to build healthy versus harmful experiences is yours, and what a power it is.
    If you are lucky enough for this world to still hold you and your children in it, you are supremely lucky in having the chance

to heal wounds. If a critical nature has driven a wedge between you and your children, then only your love and validation can undo it. You hold immense power to be able to heal those who have been harmed. This even includes children who have gone no contact. You can do the work so that the harm that was done to you does not bleed on those who did not cut you. You can project love into the world with no expectation and create a space for them to return. This is no guarantee, as pain is not so easily conquered. But to know you tried to remove a spoke from the wheel of intergenerational trauma would be a great deed.

Your children love and care about what you think so much that they stay/stayed close until the pain becomes too great, and they must protect themselves or be devoured by resentment turned to guilt. They will end up destroying themselves if they cannot be free of the guilt. This guilt is anger they won't let themselves feel and is turned inward instead. No matter how long the criticism has gone on, you have the ability to free them and yourself. It will take time. Be patient.

They think about you all the time. Every decision made in their lives has a tinge of your voice. In some cases, your voice is so powerful in their heads that there is little room for themselves. Their heads can become unsafe. Sometimes their lack of communication is not a lack of their love. It is in fact the opposite where they must give distance to maintain their love for a person they feel hurt by. You are the most important person in the definition of who they are. Make that role one of support rather than struggle. Only you can free them, unless they free themselves from you.

Start the process by working on letting things be good enough. Not everything is about a gold medal. Small wins are just as important as large ones. A strength-based model works by building on a person's inherent abilities and confidence in themselves. Breaking a person down to build them back up sounds nice, but rarely do we ever go the distance to the building back up part. If any specific instance of feedback is all they will have from you for the rest of their lives, will it serve them well?

One of the most important things in this process is to not be defensive when people bring their pain to you. If they say you hurt them, be sorry. Don't say you didn't. When they tell you a story about their childhood you can't remember, take a beat and put yourself in their shoes. How would you have felt with what they just described? Pretty uncomfortable, right? Bridges aren't all built on sunny days. It's going to be rough to hold space for a person confronting you about pain they accuse you of causing. You can do this. I believe in you.

Ultimately, they want you to deal with your own stuff. Go back to the start. Why did you push them so hard? It might have been for a good reason, but in practice it didn't always work out so well. There are reasons we don't execute our desires perfectly, and that is the emotional junk we carry. Too often we project this junk onto the ones we love most. You and only you have the power to change that behavior. You can be their hero again if you really want to. What a gift it would be for a child to have a second chance at a healthy relationship with their parent.

You don't have to agree with the decisions they make to validate why they might make them. They are your child. No one has had the chance to know them as well as you. You have had the power in this dynamic for their entire life. It is truly up to you to make it successful. You could understand them and create a safe space for them to emotionally exist so that the world could never bring them down. Or you could be the example of the dangers in this world and teach them to only rely on themselves, never asking for help.

The choice is yours for now. Good luck with your decision.

Introduction

My life experience began arguably in the late 80s or early 90s, depending on how you count the beginning (experience with or without memories). Trauma studies over the past decades alluded to the impact of the time before memory that influences our development, despite having no explicit or recall memory. This experience included the overlap of baby boomers and millennials during a time when Attention-Deficit/Hyperactivity Disorder (ADHD) was starting to be "over-diagnosed" according to the adults around me at the time. Perhaps this experience was not universal, so take my story with a grain of salt. However, it serves as a jumping-off point for this book.

It feels like science has hardly scratched the surface on the causes of certain neurodivergent diagnoses, including ADHD. This is not sufficient for my need to understand things in the context of the whole. My brain does not care for casting aside the cause of an issue, not looking beyond the genetics. I want to understand the role genetics has played in the process of development of these complex symptoms that affect a person's life so severely. I want to understand why my own brain works the way that it does.

My work as a therapist supporting clients suspected and officially diagnosed with ADHD has shown me a persistent pattern in life circumstances that seems to correlate with the development of ADHD. It has presented similarly to the avoidant symptoms of posttraumatic stress disorder (PTSD).

These avoidant symptoms seem to be so pervasive that they often are not recognized by the individual person and are a reason that research struggles to connect them to correlation or cause.

I have noticed a pattern of trauma that often leads to the development of these symptoms. It is not clear if these symptoms are PTSD, ADHD, or something that mimics either of the two, as some clients are tested and diagnosed, and others are unable to be tested. A pervasive, internalized voice of a caretaker makes the mind an unsafe place for the person with ADHD so that they spend most of their waking time attempting to escape it and are sometimes unaware this behavior is even happening until discussed.

In this book, I will explain my understanding of circumstances that have led to the difficulty in diagnosis and treatment of ADHD. This difficulty may be due to a lack of knowledge in the development of the disorder. I will discuss pervasive characteristics in caretakers that lead to these negative internalized voices, the cycle of abuse often associated with this developing into PTSD (causing complex PTSD), and thus leading to the collection of symptoms we label ADHD.

I also explore maladaptive coping strategies used by many individuals to manage these symptoms, discuss the possible origins in their development, and follow up with identifying healthy and adaptive strategies to manage and combat the origins of these symptoms. I will also address barriers to treatment and relief based on issues of cost, waitlists, government regulation, and access to care to develop a new treatment direction.

Why bother writing this book? I don't know. I feel selfish having information in my head that could help others, and I struggle with the limitations of passing on this knowledge a single person at a time. I have ADHD and was not diagnosed until the age of 37. I went through life not understanding why everything was so hard and believing myself to be lazy. I know I cannot prevent the pain of others, which was my early mistake in getting into this field in the first place. However, maybe I can help others not have to struggle with the guilt and shame of it all and be a voice that calls to the powers that be to research the crap out of this thing and finally find a way to utilize the skills ADHD does give us instead of being punished for not being able to be neurotypical without pain and suffering.

I want to be able to share these ideas with people. The information can help those who are struggling while also calling for action from society. Direct research in this area of psychology is drastically underrepresented. Much of the research I cite is adjacent to the major issues I see without addressing them. Too often, genetics is the end point of finding a cause rather than a reason to look further. Here, I challenge science to understand the genetics as I point to the behaviors in many of these cases of ADHD during childhood development. People are hurting and unheard, and by working together, we can give them voice.

Trigger Warning: mentioning domestic violence, abuse, strong analogies

Part I: Narcissism

Chapter 1
Highly Critical Parents

Our introduction to the world is through our parents. They are our first relationships. These foundational relationships often have echoing patterns through the rest of our lives, for good and bad. They're the blueprint for how we respond to the world. I can't tell you how often people will say that they don't want to dwell on the past or talk about what happened in childhood or blame their parents for what is happening in their lives today. That's all well and good, and there are types of therapy that can support that, (such as existentialism-based therapy), but a holistic approach similar to Gestalt therapy also follows these beliefs with consideration for how the past affects the here and now.

Gestalt psychology talks about how the whole is greater than the sum of its parts. We are the culmination of every experience and decision that was ever made for us and that we ever made for ourselves. The outcomes of these decisions have everything to do with our desire to repeat or avoid them. Our core belief systems are often based on what has and has not worked and how well those experiences harmonize with any given belief system in the authority figures around us. We are greater than the sum of our experiences, but if any one strong enough experience was different, then we also would be different.

The start of our life and experiences is through the mirrored connection with a caretaker. We look to them for reassurance to know whether something we're doing is going to be okay. We look to them for comfort when things are not okay. We look to them for praise when things go well through our choices and autonomy. This is the exact aspect of the relationship that is often wounded by a critical parent. Most experiments in child development look to the relationship between the child and the caretaker as a measure of positive or negative outcome. A secure relationship leads to many positives, such as resiliency, autonomy, confidence, and healthy relationships with others. The opposite can be true of insecure attachments.

A highly critical parent, as I will describe throughout this book, is a parent whose criticism outweighs any positive reinforcement to a point where it causes specific responses from the child [1], [2]. Like PTSD, what is traumatic to one child might not be traumatic to another. A parent saying they were no harder on [insert person here] does not excuse said parent from the wounds that were caused in the child who was wounded. A highly critical parent may have an anxious-ambivalent, dismissive-avoidant, or fearful-avoidant attachment with the child. These are all insecure attachment styles.

An anxious-ambivalent attachment style is often overbearing. The parent in this attachment is engrossed in the child's life and can sometimes be called a helicopter parent. This attachment style has a push/pull modality to it. The parent is either all-in on the child's life and decisions or completely ambivalent to their needs. This ambivalence can be a form of emotional resentment taken out on the child for rejecting the parent. The overbearing nature of the push/pull dynamic is often the one that has outspoken criticism or can also provide encouragement at times. We will discuss later in cycles of abuse how this can be both at separate times of the cycle.

The dismissive-avoidant attachment style is when the parent is often disinterested or withholding affection when the child seeks it. The dismissive parent might provide just enough emotional support to keep the child from seeking other sources. The type of love from these insecure attachments can very much feel conditional, as it often is. Love is replaced with praise which requires performance. Neglect is displayed as punishment for failure to meet expectations. A problem with these expectations in a dismissive attachment style is that they often move so that you can never meet them. We will discuss this more in the later chapter on the narcissistic abuse cycle.

The fearful-avoidant attachment style is from the parent who responds to the child in a way that instills fear. These types of relationships are often where there are more severe aspects of emotional abuse and outright unacceptable behaviors. This is also the attachment style in which relationships with parents can become emotionally incestuous. Often the relationship with one parent as their emotional support child evokes fear of failure and the need to fix an adult's problem as a child. It can also lead to jealousy and competition/resentment from the other parent, who has been replaced in this dynamic. Either way leads to a child having too much emotional responsibility for adults and a fearful response in failure.

Any of these attachment styles can come from a highly critical parent. "Highly," as used here, refers to the severity of the criticism. A highly resilient child may be emotionally unbothered by their parent's push with little to no positive encouragement and might not consider this parent highly critical. Meanwhile, another child might not be able to emotionally withstand even a quarter of what the first child may need to perform. "Highly" in this case is subjective based on the response of the child and can be predicted based on protective factors; a child with a strong sense of self, a good support system, and healthy coping skills will not be hindered by criticism.

Alternatively, a child who has more risk factors might have less of a sense of self, lower self-efficacy, little to no support system, a lack of boundaries, and unhealthy coping skills. This development pattern can be caused by the attachment and parenting style provided to the child. In some cases, "highly" might refer to a ratio of 3:1 criticism to compliments. Children who have already been affected by highly critical parenting might have a severe reaction even to 1:1 criticism to compliments, ignoring the compliment and only focusing on the criticism. These criticisms can be spoken or withheld.

I would say that criticism is not only the spoken or identified failure to reach an expectation. It can also be negative in the reduction of interaction with a child. The removal of positive reinforcement can be a negative experience for a child when they look with pride to a caretaker and receive nothing in return. Mirroring is described in much of the child development literature. It is when a parent matches the energy of the child. Mirroring is how we encode our brains to understand the world and how we fit in it. Feeling happy at times when the parent responds with happiness enhances said happiness. Feeling joyful when a parent is upset is confusing and leads to more negative feelings. Neglectful reinforcement is often relayed by ambivalent or dismissive parents. It can have just as much of an effect on the child as critical responses [3].

Sometimes a critical parent is critical due to their own traumas or how they might have been taught, or not taught, to be a parent. A critical parent might feel resentment toward their children for what the parent must give up or even for what the child is afforded that they were not able to receive. In some instances, the trauma of the parent has led to personality disorders. Narcissism, often representing narcissistic personality disorder, though they are *not* the same, is the type of critical parenting that I will most often be referencing through this book. It is not the only type of highly critical parent, and not all highly critical parents reach the diagnostic criteria for narcissistic personality disorder. However, for the specific mechanisms that I will be discussing, narcissism fits the description best and seems most well-known.

We know the signs of being raised by a highly critical parent. They are similar to those of a narcissistic parent, if not the same. The degree of severity might be different due to the level of behavior from the parent or the strength of defense from the child. Children of highly critical parents, and even later as adults, can have the following signs of this early experience: difficulty trusting yourself, hard time taking on challenges, difficulty bouncing back from mistakes, perfectionism, long time to complete tasks, apologize frequently, feel defensive, disbelieve people like you, difficulty taking compliments, social anxiety, harsh inner critic, prone to depression, critical of others, strained sibling relationships, overthink, and need to prove yourself [4].

I will primarily focus on highly critical parenting through the lens of narcissism throughout the rest of the book, in relation to trauma and ADHD. This style of parenting is characterized by grandiosity, a need for others to like them, and a lack of empathy to differing degrees. This is not to say they are not capable of empathy, but similarly to antisocial personality disorder, they will put themselves first to differing levels of the dark triad. Narcissism can be boiled down to an intense need for validation from the world to combat the deep-seated feelings of inadequacy.

I want to be careful here in the discussion of personality disorders, as they carry a strong negative connotation with them in society. It is rare that people would often knowingly seek out these types of behaviors in friends or partners. I don't want to disparage or glorify these traits, as not every person suffering from them is malignant, but some can be. So, I want to express the need to stay safe, utilizing healthy boundaries and validation rather than codependent behaviors.

The maladaptive traits of these disorders are often difficult for even therapists to manage and maintain healthy boundaries. Therapists are taught to sense how each disorder makes them personally feel and to trust their gut (and verify later) about the subtle and often charming ways in which the maladaptive traits test boundaries to get needs met. Later, I will teach you some boundary setting skills to manage these issues.

So often, we discuss the braggadocious nature of the narcissist and find distaste in their seeking of approval that we forget a person seeking approval is often lacking esteem. Narcissists are emotionally fragile people and the reason the word "weak" is weaponized in toxic masculinity. Use of "weak" is a projection of their own internal fear. A narcissist is so terrified of not being good enough or being perceived as weak that they will chase the validation of others to their own detriment and often while stepping on those they appear to hold close.

The internalized and vicious voice in their head is often only seen by their children, who we label as the scapegoat or golden child. It is one of the signs of having a highly critical parent. A narcissist would seem to have a highly critical parent, or a highly permissive parent whose sporadic attempts at correction feel highly critical to the narcissist. If you want to understand how a narcissist feels and thinks on the inside, listen to their victims, who have had these emotions projected onto them and were gaslit into adopting these emotions.

The narcissist is seeking validation from their caretakers, or anyone who will see them, to be able to know that they are good enough. I tend to imagine an elementary-aged child excitedly bringing a picture home from school and being derided by a parent for some reason or another, which takes that joy and turns it to shame in a single moment. This image is what gives me the empathy needed to treat the narcissist with compassion. It does not necessarily reflect the actual cause of this disorder.

In the next chapter, I will go into more depth about this specific disorder.

Chapter 2
Narcissism

I want to start off this chapter by simply saying that not all narcissists are malignant or intentionally harmful. In fact, this is the most complicated question I receive all the time: Do they know what they are doing when they hurt me? Yes, no, and it depends on their level of emotional intelligence. The difficult part of living around or being under the power of a narcissist is that the rules are constantly changing for reasons that are not clear and often attributed to the person failing to follow these rules as being not smart enough to figure them out. This is not the case.

The world of narcissism is dictated by emotion and emotional need. This can be long-term planning or moment-by-moment depending on the level of stress and strength of the need for validation. At times, a narcissist will make rules that contradict something they have said recently. Their answer? You just can't understand. What you and they are struggling to understand is the shifting landscape of their internal sense of self. The rules are meant to keep them above you and all others in the attempt to reach validation.

The honest answer to these rules is since it is based on emotion, it can also affect their memory of events and past dictation of rules. Studies have shown this same effect of emotion on memory in eyewitness accuracy [5], [6]. Sometimes they know they are lying and other times they genuinely believe there is no difference in the rulings they are making. Challenging this often would lead to the use of DARVO, or Deny, Attack, and Reverse Victim and Offender. DARVO is the response if you were to ever confront or try to "take down" a narcissistic person. It is a defense mechanism that is not always conscious.

Narcissists are often referred to as difficult people. They can be hard to love without taking on your own internalized damage of feeling not good enough or even stupid. The level to which they understand their own behavior is difficult to judge due to the issues of grandiosity and deceit. If you back them into a corner about how they harmed you, you might be called too sensitive, or they say they did not mean it, so you should forgive them. Question if they realize how mean and intentional their behavior feels, and they might blame your behavior for making them act that way. They agree with strength. Thus, a strength-based model can help in communicating with them. We will discuss that more later in the healing and boundaries section.

The life of a narcissist is not one to be envied. This is part of the reason we end up with billionaires. How much is enough? It is hard to measure enough with a hole in your bucket. The childhood of a narcissist would certainly be filled with criticism beyond what could be tolerated, creating such a hole. The wounds that lead to personality issues often happen at an early age when our personalities are still forming. Developmental psychology puts this around seven years old, and personality stays consistent through the lifespan. This is also why issues in personality often are so difficult to change and can instead be redirected or channeled into healthier behaviors.

Imagine us as a bucket meant to hold esteem. Positive feedback fills this bucket, and negative feedback can empty the bucket. As I stated before, narcissism can form during development when a hole is placed in the bucket of the self, where we carry our self-esteem. Narcissists lose esteem without the continual addition of positive feedback due to an abundance of harmful feedback in childhood. Some examples that lead to this include children having to find a switch to be punished with or not being allowed to come home with a 98% on a test. It would be a complex or chronic trauma made up of many of these smaller traumas, or t's ("little t's"), that wear on the soul like the Colorado River on the Grand Canyon. Each story of these traumas is so complex due to the varying nature of the culmination of traumas and difficulty in remembering individual instances. No brush can paint all experience, but as humans we react in similar ways to similar pain.

As I have said, the life of a narcissist is not easy and does not get easier later. The bucket has a hole, and both the bucket and the hole only grow as the narcissist gains success in life. Parenthood for a narcissist is incredibly difficult and leads to a lot of traumas for the entire family. It is pervasive and does not only affect the person afflicted. A child is an extension of the narcissistic self. They are meant to be reflections of the narcissist. Success is required. Love is a luxury to be earned. Children will thrive if they accept their role within the system. Others will struggle if they have an innate sense of justice. The narcissist wants their children to succeed, but there is a catch to this goal.

The child best not dare challenge the security of the narcissist's feelings of adequacy. *Codependency enters the ring.* While often mistaken as two people being overly reliant on each other, codependency is an intolerance of others' emotions, especially when they do not match your own. Think of a villain's henchmen laughing a little too long and the negative response from the boss. Or a parent asking why a child is sad or crying and trying to invalidate away those feelings since they are uncomfortable to the parent. The same goes for the success and celebration of the child of a narcissist.

There are many names for the "types of narcissism." Some are more malicious, some less threatening. The key is their intent, need, and how they treat others. The more classical kind is typically simplified as narcissism when we discuss it: overt narcissism. Overt narcissists will parent with direct criticism and transactional love. Another form is covert narcissism. Covert narcissists are often described as martyrs. They tend to use guilt and shame through sacrifice to get their needs met. Similar in nature, communal narcissists, sometimes called white knights, have their needs met through sacrifice. They gain admiration through the actions they do that seem altruistic. The flaw in this armor is the anger they display when they are not allowed to help.

The narcissist's highly critical nature is so pervasive to children that it can become an internalized voice inside their head. The problem with this is often that voices for those who have internal monologues sound the same tonally. Later in life when I treat these clients, they will describe the voice as their own until they answer a few questions:

- Do you think you were born this critical of yourself?
- Where might you have learned to speak like this?
- Whose verbiage is the language in?
- Was there ever a highly critical person in your life that might have sounded like the one in your head?

This is the pervasive nature of narcissism. It can start with one person struggling emotionally to feel good enough and their maladaptive coping skills taking it out on everyone else to the point that their own internal monologue is implanted in other people's heads. It can even transcend generations through intergenerational trauma. I often see clients who can be three generations from the identified narcissist and still feel the telltale effects of self-doubt and delusional guilt.

Intergenerational trauma and historical trauma are important to understand in this context. If you are unaware, intergenerational trauma is handed down through family lines genetically and through behaviors and beliefs in raising children. Responses to trauma are unintentionally taught even when the trauma is no longer present. Historical trauma is a trauma that affected everyone at a particular time in history. Examples of this would include WWI, WWII, Korea, Vietnam, 9/11, George Floyd, and so many others. I sometimes jokingly (but not so jokingly) mention Harambe as a historical trauma due to the older generations identifying with the person who shot him to save the child, and the younger generations identifying as the problem to be shot.

Chemically toxic environments added onto the historical and intergenerational traumas of these times that could have led to so much negativity, trauma, and narcissism. Leaded gasoline in the US was not fully phased out until 1996. However, someone born before 1979 has 95% more lead poisoning than someone born after 1996. Lead had a serious effect on adult personality within the Big 5 personality traits, ultimately resulting in a less mature personality in adulthood [7], which may have had a strong influence on parenting. Most parents today were born during the time of lead poisoning in childhood. This correlation is not necessarily a cause, as none of what I am saying is cause and effect but rather circumstantially related at the very least.

How do I spot a narcissist? One of the telltale signs for me is what I call a moving target. This could also be called moving the goal post and often includes gaslighting. I call it a moving target because it is often vague enough that it can be hard to aim toward, unlike a goal post. It tends to play out with the person proposing a goal or idea to me, and in reflective listening they keep modifying it to such a degree it feels like a game of three-card monte. However, there are many other ways to spot a narcissist.

I used to joke with colleagues that anyone who knocks on a door with the "shave and a haircut" pattern is often a difficult person. I *may* have used more colorful language. This is due to the process of knocking on a door. It is a boundary. They have not passed said boundary. And yet, this knock often expects a playful response of "two bits." They are unaware if you accept this playful game, and you are unaware of who is on the other side of the door. Non-consensual performative expectation (let us call it the NCPE) is a key check that a narcissist will make. You will not like their response if you do not respond correctly unless you are a confrontational person. The person who does not play the NCPE may be targeted as the narcissistic scapegoat.

The fastest way to anger a narcissist, short of calling them inferior, is to not play their games. This ignites an anger in them due to you now being a threat outside of their control. It can start with picking on you about not playing along. It can then poke and prod the same spot over and over to wound you, remarking on your sensitivity when you protest. This anger is what I refer to as abusive anger. It does not alleviate. It is simply cathartic. By taking out their frustration on the scapegoat, some narcissists learn that the rest of their behavior can be more pro-social. They need you more than you need them in these relationships.

Understand a few things about having a relationship with a narcissist. You are not going to cure them. You can only protect yourself and your needs in the process of a relationship with them. If you are the scapegoat, leave. Someone else will fill your place. If you are in a relationship with a non-malicious narcissist and you can understand their limitations emotionally without taking things personally, the relationship might continue. It won't be perfect. Sometimes the best way to shut down a narcissist is to validate that you do not understand what they are trying to get from you, but they are going about it the wrong way. It would be best to revisit this when you are both in a better emotional space. Then stop engaging. Maybe listen and validate, but don't argue. If things become unsafe, leave or call 911. Every person is different, so this is an example and not advice. Sometimes nothing will work and being safe is the only option.

It's common for the day after a harmful event the narcissist (or even a lot of people with some maladaptive personality traits) will act like nothing ever happened. I will discuss more options for this later in the boundary chapter. Don't expect an apology due to the emotionally vulnerable place a person has to go to give a proper one. We often see politicians and the like giving what people call non-apologies. These are statements like "I'm sorry if" or "I didn't know you were that sensitive." Any statement that is about how you perceived or felt something versus them trying to take responsibility for hurting you is not an apology.

As a final note to this chapter, be careful in labeling people as narcissists, especially online. There are nuances to some of these issues, and due to the pervasiveness of the behaviors, other disorders can look narcissistic. Specifically, I have noticed autistic people and most people with ADHD have narcissistic-like symptoms (or airs of narcissism). The difference often lies in the intent. Victims of narcissists can often trigger other victims of narcissists due to what I call narcissist light behaviors. This is because they often do not have the malignant intent.

In the spirit of Dan Povenmire's Doofenshmirtz line about having a nickel for every time something happens, I too can relate that although not rich I am surprised with how often a spouse has been sent to me for therapy when they asked a narcissistic partner to go to couples counseling. Even though it's not a lot, it's still odd to see it as much as I have. Couples issues cannot be solved through individual therapy alone, and the partner would do better to go to therapy *with* them as I teach them both boundaries and how to protect against emotional harm.

Chapter 3
The Narcissistic Abuse Cycle

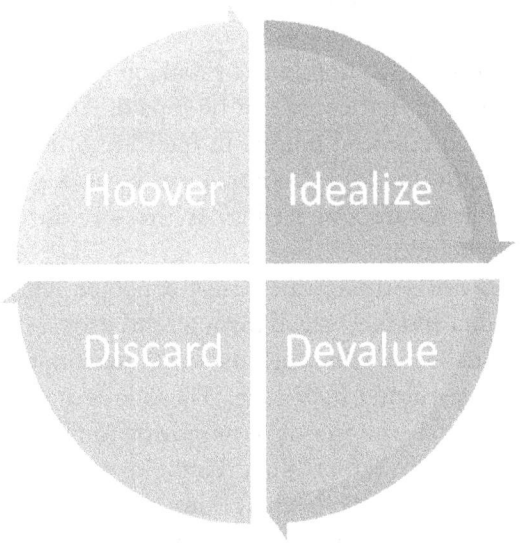

The critical voice is implanted in the mind of the targets of narcissistic abuse through what I have seen described as the Narcissistic Abuse Cycle (NAC). This version is similar and yet different to Lenore E. Walker's Cycle of Abuse [8]. Her cycle also has four stages: Tension building, Incident, Reconciliation, and Calm, whereas the version that I would prefer to utilize labels the stages Idealize, Devalue, Discard, and Hoover. The origin of these terms seems unclear other than the common use of Hoovering to mean vacuuming in the UK. Walker's cycle is closer in tone to that of the cycle of abuse and is named Walker's Cycle of Abuse, which I will discuss in a later chapter. For now, I will refer to the latter mentioned cycle.

The first phase, Idealizing, is important here as it is often the answer to the question "why did I put up with this for so long" or comparable questions. The idealization phase could be more commonly referred to as love bombing. This is a phase that carries more weight today, as it is more widely mentioned. Love bombing is understood to be part of the initial stages of an abusive relationship in which the abuser is building what I tend to refer to as emotional equity. They are banking goodwill for later when the cycle shifts as it always has for them. A good example of this is love bombing or making grand gestures early in the relationship that could not be repaid. An average person who has not experienced trauma in their life often leaves when a person might be love bombing or idealizing due to the uncomfortable nature and feeling, as this amount of attention can be overwhelming.

This is not as much the case for people who have been through trauma and feel valued through this process. It is normal in transactional love relationships for a person to give more when you have earned their love. These love bombing phases seem more like a one-to-one comparison on how much this person values you rather than banking goodwill for when kindness is unsustainable later. If something was truly given in love, it is given freely without expectation of return and thus has no resentment attached, ever. The opposite is true for transactional love, and it can be a hard pill to swallow if you are now realizing during the reading of this book that some of the love given was conditional. Therapy might be an important part of any realization found through the chapters of this book.

The Idealization phase is completely conditional like a payday loan. The conditions are purposefully hidden in the fine print, only to be shown when it is time to collect. A rule of thumb that I often use is 3:1. No person should give more than three times to each one you are returning and vice versa. This is not intended to make the love conditional but rather track when any relationship is becoming dangerously unbalanced and ripe for abuse. Abusers will often give more in the beginning of the relationship, as previously mentioned to be love bombing, and less later in the relationship. A person who often gives might give too much out of gratitude to a person who is only willing to take.

The next stage is Devaluing. You could also label devaluing as nitpicking. Storylines on infatuation show this stage as the one in which all the flaws are starting to be noticed by the once-enamored lovers. In the NAC, devaluing has a purpose. As the narcissist, I would have built my fortune and stockpiled gold before crashing the economy. If you are less valuable when it comes time to return the favors or repay the debts, it can often feel as though those debts have become insurmountable. The narcissist has placed a finger on the scale during their measurement and uses that same finger to lift the scale on the other side when it comes time to measure your contribution.

I warn all my clients who are used to transactional love and unintentionally build this emotional equity with others that there is no guarantee of return. Everything that is given must be given freely. I then say the same joke each time as I ask what they will do when the narcissist does not return the value given? Will you break their legs as if you are in the mob? The answer is of course no, and we learn a lesson to not give what we cannot afford to lose without resentment.

The Devalue phase is also referenced when a person might want to leave the relationship. This is where the abuser will tell a person that no one else will treat them kindly and that they are lucky to have been cared for so well. The overvaluing of the Idealization phase is a sneaky form of devaluing. Small acts of kindness in the early days of a relationship feel much larger. The acts performed in the Idealization phase have more value than the same acts returned later. If the true value of the love bombing were viewed in the context of the entire relationship, it might not have been accepted knowing what was required as payment later. This behavior is not an honest investment.

If you're upside down in a loan and in so much debt you can never repay, many people would look to bankruptcy. The narcissist will try to never push you so far that you declare this, or their investment is lost. You have the power to walk away, even with nothing if necessary. They cannot afford to lose all the effort they have put into you at this point. It is often when the target of the narcissist finally says "I'll do it myself" that the narcissist magically takes care of whatever it was they were refusing to help with and devalued you over previously. This is no guarantee. It can happen this way, or they can wait for things to get worse and for you to need them more while they swoop in and devalue more. Self-esteem is the best defense here. You are not a burden. Therapy can help develop this defense.

This is where a narcissist will punish you in the Discard phase. They will discard you for someone else and begin the love bombing process on someone to hurt you. The narcissist does not do this freely. The adulation given to the narcissist by this new person was like what you might have given the narcissist in response to your love bombing or idealization phase. The narcissist does not give anything away for free. They were taking their share all along while convincing you it was charity. The narcissist utilizes a new supply of validation to sustain them through this phase.

This is where the transactional aspect of the relationship becomes fully apparent. The narcissist will throw a person/relationship away when it is not suiting them. Often this comes after having asked for something from the narcissist and especially after reminding them of the goodwill you had cultivated previously. They don't want to be reminded of this and will often engage in what Freud called reaction formation, where they increase resistance and change the narrative.

The reaction formation used in this moment is that they have not done enough for you, and they are not enough for you in the relationship. The narcissist will then begin the process of throwing the relationship away, as it has made them feel worthless and hints at their insufficiency. They may even begin gaslighting in this phase, noting all they have done and accusing you of being selfish or ungrateful. The Discard phase of the cycle is often during a time when the narcissist is wounded or feels as though they are doing everything they can, and it is not enough. Thus, the Discard phase is more about the narcissist's emotions about themself rather than the target of their ire.

No relationship should be able to fall apart when asking for support. "No" should always be an acceptable answer to a request. The narcissist does not view "no" as an option here and thus must escape the relationship. The average person should be able to say "no" to something they do not want to do. This would look poor on the narcissist, and you can see this through the acrobatics with which they use to convince you of anything. Gaslighting is about convincing you that you are okay with their request, or your view is so outlandish that it should be an exception. "No" is a much better option.

The Discard phase is often how a narcissist will punish you, as I have said before. The process by which they practice this punishment is often labeled as DARVO (see Chapter 2). The DARVO pattern is used regularly in negative interactions with a person who is narcissistic. Their sense of self-worth cannot admit to having done something that hurt another person or was not good in some way that they need to utilize the reaction formation mentioned above. This process allows them to remain inherently good enough while casting the victim into the role of the person who is really at fault. We see this happen often in the court systems and before the #MeToo movement. Rape culture was a huge proponent of this mentality in trying to protect "good, young men" from accusations that would harm their future.

The paradoxical viewpoints are common among this population of toxically masculine men. You must not be weak, but weakness is so scary that only delusion can save you. You must take what you want, but it is the fault of the victim for not protecting that thing more. You must follow the rules and climb the ladder through merit, but the friend of the boss gets the position they are not qualified for. The rules are unjust and based on the momentary need of the most sensitive person: the narcissist.

I believe something specific happens in this cycle between this phase and the next, specifically with the development of Complex Posttraumatic Stress disorder (CPTSD) and ADHD. It would seem through my understanding and experience in treating these conditions that they often skip phase four and return to phase one at this point due to fear of losing the relationship with the narcissist. I will discuss later an aspect of neurodivergent reaction called Rejection Sensitive Dysphoria. The dysphoria from the mere idea of rejection is enough for people with ADHD or CPTSD to be unable to risk losing the relationship and thus "fall in line" for the narcissist before ever reaching phase four.

Phase four is called Hoovering or reconciliation. Hoovering is an interesting term that I prefer over reconciliation due to the imagery it evokes. I can't find the origin of the term in use regarding personality disorders, but it is used commonly across literature that describes this phase of the cycle specific to abuse from personality disorders and even more specifically narcissism. Hoovering is the attempt to bring a person back into a relationship with a narcissist. It tends to begin following the rejection or perceived rejection of the narcissist by anyone.

The term Hoovering comes from the UK due to its implications toward the nature of a vacuum. The attempt to suck back in the target of the narcissist is not so often direct and can be difficult to fully identify purposefully. A chance meeting or an accidental text or phone call can open the door to conversation between two people who might not be talking. Alienation by people around a person might cause them to feel lonely enough that they return to the narcissist willingly. Family members randomly reminiscing about a past narcissist and all the good they had done might spark nostalgia and a desire to return to them or reach out. As I have seen in my years working with survivors of these relationships, much of this is planned and purposeful.

The narcissist can also be much more direct in the process of Hoovering. Examples of this would be a person calling or texting incessantly over the course of a brief period of up to a week or more. Descriptions of these abusive behaviors often include the narcissistic person changing their number to avoid being blocked and creating new emails to bombard their target. The goal is to overwhelm the person and push them into a state of emotional instability or fight or flight mode. A person cannot access rational thought in this state due to our emotional center of the brain being in control when we are in survival mode. We don't have access to the prefrontal cortex or rational thought at these times unless much therapy has been had.

Hoovering often entails gaslighting and getting the target to succumb to the abuse and wanting it to stop or wanting to stop being "difficult" for the narcissist. The bait of phase one is an alluring reward in acquiescing to the narcissist's demands. Hoovering in this way is often like some interrogation techniques that tell the target all they must do to end the pain and be treated well is give the interrogator what they want. "You have the power to stop this at any time" or "I don't know why you make me do this to you." These are sinister statements meant to transfer blame while appearing as if they are taking pity on you. They are emotionally digging fingers into your ribs while helping you to stand again.

How long does the NAC last? That's a difficult yet simple question to answer. It lasts until you return to where the narcissist wants you in a relationship or until they get bored and move on to other targets. They don't typically get bored easily or move on quickly, which can be distressing for anyone at the mercy of the narcissist. Returning by design is easier in the short term. It meets the need of the narcissist to not be abandoned and to see themself as good enough despite the incredible effort it takes to maintain this state.

The return to phase one is where they recognize they may have pushed this cycle too hard and too fast. They realize the need to build you and the relationship up before they can exert more pressure. The beginning of each cycle feels almost good due to the exploitation of the sense of relief. Feeling good and feeling relief are different but often construed to mean the same thing, especially in the addiction world. Phase one is comfort and a pat on the back with the goal of preparing you to be able to take more in this next round.

Chapter 4
The Effects of the Narcissistic Abuse Cycle

The NAC has so many effects on the brain and body due to the extreme nature of the process by which it works. It pushes an intended victim into a state of fear and survival mode where emotions are high. The longer and more often a person is in this state, the easier and more often they will enter this state. This process can even become automatic over time. The short-term effects of the NAC are like crawling out of a warzone: confusion, headaches, dizziness, and poor memory for unidentifiable reasons. Physical pain and symptoms related to somatic disorders can also be common.

The effects are meant to cause confusion and a form of paralysis to hinder the ability to escape from the relationship or reduce the resistance to Hoovering. They continue to cause difficulty concentrating and regulating emotion, can disorient and affect decision making, and can limit access to problem solving and critical thinking skills [9]. These symptoms can be short term and last longer depending on the exposure to the NAC. As the abuse continues, the behaviors are more integrated into the self and affect areas such as self-esteem or self-efficacy. The above reference also lists these longer-term effects: "low self-esteem and self-worth, anxiety and/or depression, PTSD, difficulty forming trusting relationships, and feelings of shame and guilt" [9].

Multiple articles state that the NAC also causes longer term effects that are similar in people currently trapped in an NAC and people who have escaped it. The effects last past the imposition of the abuse. Results like this seem adjacent to other studies on cognitive inflexibility in addiction, OCD [10], and religious fundamentalism [11]. Cognitive flexibility and openness are important to the ability of the brain to change a person's belief structures, whereas the NAC works completely against the ideas of cognitive flexibility and openness, as often seen in cult mentalities.

It is a large leap to make that the NAC is a factor in the development of cognitive inflexibility and reduced openness, however it does seem relevant to the development of trauma disorders like PTSD, CPTSD, OCD, and in my belief ADHD, which I will discuss in a later chapter. However, we do know of the long-term effects of the NAC in adults regardless of whether it is caused by brain damage or not. We also have seen in past studies that increased cortisol levels in the brain for an extended period can have a lasting effect on the development of the limbic system (emotional center of the brain).

These aspects of cognitive limitation, alone or in combination, can influence the limitations of those with traumatic pasts. There seems to be a wealth of support for the effect of stress on the developing brain in limiting the volume of the hippocampus and affecting the amygdala and prefrontal cortex. Overexposure to cortisol has shown the ability to kill brain cells, and stress leads to functional atrophy [12]. These issues similarly present in individuals who are subject to the NAC, are part of the development of maladaptive patterns that are strongly associated with changes in the physical structure of the brain, and persistent behavioral/cognitive changes.

Regardless of the possible causes and effects or reasons for all these developments, science has shown a specific set of maladaptive responses in people who have been subjected to the NAC. Below is a list of traits in adult children of narcissists [13]:

- Low self-esteem
- Perfectionism
- Anxiety and depression
- Chronic self-blame
- Identity issues
- Codependency
- Difficulty setting and enforcing boundaries
- Emotional dysregulation
- Hypervigilance and sensitivity to criticism
- People-pleasing tendencies and difficulty expressing needs
- Trouble identifying and expressing emotions
- Physical health issues
- Chronic self-doubt and insecurity
- Difficulty trusting others and forming relationships
- Resilience and strength

These responses stem from the heightened state of emotional stress that affects the functionality of the limbic system, including confusion, cognitive dissonance, and memory issues (hippocampus) and an effect on the amygdala, which is known for controlling basic physiological function [14] and the four F's: fight, flight, food, and sex. The abuse cycle keeps a person in this survival mode with increased cortisol levels.

Nearly every paper on this subject quotes Daniel Goleman's c.1995 work *Emotional Intelligence* [15]. These references tend to point out the changes made by cortisol in the brain specifically to the hippocampus and the need of the hippocampus to properly interpret the world. This process is disrupted through the NAC. Our hippocampus is limited in its growth and thus limits our ability to accurately take in the world around us. This leads to maladaptive patterns in order to exist in a world that would make no sense if our brain was not creative enough to adapt to the contradictory rules of a narcissist using our own rationalizations.

As mentioned before, survivors of this type of abuse are often very self-deprecating to the point that it might be uncomfortable to hear them describe themselves. It can feel like an act that they are beating themselves up to this extent, however this is due to the behavior used to please their abuser, called fawning. We have discussed the fight or flight response earlier. Well, that is only part of it. The full description is fight, flight, freeze, or fawn. Fight and flight are the obvious and often first responses to danger. Freezing is what happens when neither of those two are viable. Fawning happens after continuous abuse when freezing no longer works.

What would you do in a case where you cannot fight, you cannot run, and just taking it is too much? Perhaps like many others have learned, you might notice the emotions of the people around you and start to try and placate them. You might start to perform in a way that meets the need of the abuser or calls for sympathy from a witness. This behavior happens so often that you become good at detecting minor changes in the moods of the people around you before they are even aware of it, like an emotional support child/person. Fawning becomes so automatic that often you will gaslight yourself into believing everything is your fault to avoid confrontation.

Fawning is how a person learns to survive when they live near an emotional powder keg. An example might be the fundie baby voice. Fawning does not come across as desirable to the average person. It tends to come across as off, immature, and dissonant, which is why it can be so uncomfortable to hear. A person in tune with their emotions can sense this dissonance easily and might want to escape it. Fawning behavior is the goal of grooming for this reason. It prevents real help for the victims of the abuser and can often force the fawning person into service to help recruit new targets.

A person can heal from these traumas and even learn to no longer mask or fawn. They might be able to get into touch with their emotions once again. A person could have healthy relationships and marry a partner that is nothing like previous abusers. However, this is where a secondary issue can start. A long-lasting effect of abuse in childhood is that the average person cannot fathom that anyone, let alone a parent, would do some of these awful things to a child. Many times, I have had clients discuss how their in-laws invalidated their stories due to disbelief and wanting to believe better in humanity.

I believe this is due in part to the empathetic brain putting a person in the shoes of the perpetrator or actor. Healthy people can't see themselves committing these traumas to the people standing in front of them and thus cannot fathom it to be true. Even worse could be that the in-law can empathize with the actor and even blame the survivor for what happened. We see this often when politicians, judges, law enforcement, DAs, and people in power want to save the young man who might have "made a mistake" by viciously taking away the opportunity of consent from another human being. Convicted rapists are given probation, avoid the registry, and are even able to work with children again.

When a survivor speaks out, we must believe them and follow the process for justice. As Judith Herman discusses in *Truth and Recovery*, it is not often about the punishment but the validation of society agreeing what had happened was wrong [16]. The process of this type of trauma makes people not even believe in themselves. Now add in the process of a loved one questioning, "are you sure?" Or a legal system delaying the proceedings or not charging an individual. The effects of the

NAC are worsened when our society takes part in the invalidation. The process can be trauma inducing.

Part II: Trauma

Chapter 5
Cycle of Abuse

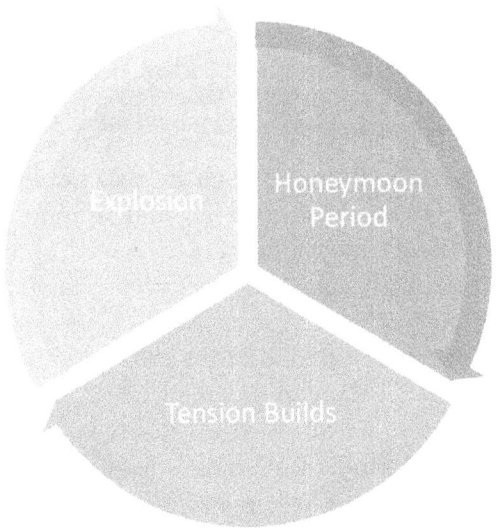

The cycle of abuse, often associated with PTSD, is similar in many ways to the NAC, except that it is missing the phase of Hoovering and the names are slightly different. You might notice how the Honeymoon phase of this cycle is remarkably like the Idealization phase of the NAC. This is due to their similar purposes in the cycles. They are the time that is so good, much better than most people who would tolerate these cycles believe they deserve (however untrue that might be). Likewise, the Tension Building (Frustration) phase is like the Devaluing phase, and the Explosion phase is like the Discarding phase.

Both cycles are about the abusive patterns within relationships rather than single experience traumas. In a later chapter, I will discuss more the little t's of these relational traumas and the effect they have in that specific area of complex PTSD. Survivors of this type of abuse go through these cycles so many times that their limbic system gets pretty accurate at predicting the cycle, despite the conscious brain not necessarily knowing what is happening or what to expect short of "danger."

A honeymoon period is common in the first three months or so of any relationship. This is when you are getting to know someone, and everything seems novel and interesting. Couples tend to fight less during this phase and are often more giving and loving to woo their new partner. This phase happening once at the start of a relationship is normal and should be expected. It is not typically love bombing, though it *would* be if the behavior were happening so frequently that it would be impossible to keep up and there was an expectation of repayment at some point. We will discuss boundaries and an effective way to avoid this in a later chapter.

The Honeymoon period of the cycle of abuse is different in that it happens regularly to the point where you could almost set your watch to it, if your watch had three phases. There is a calculation that the limbic system does for us through this cycle when you have been through it enough times. The longer the Honeymoon period, the longer the Tension Building or Frustration period, the worse and more dangerous the Explosive period will be. The Frustration period is waiting for the other shoe to drop. The Explosive period is the other shoe dropping. This would be the reason that the Honeymoon period is not enjoyable. That, and the person being nice to you was also very recently unstable and outright abusive.

The Honeymoon period is both the beginning and end phase of the abusive cycle. It is what some would refer to as reconciliation, but it is also the time when love bombing occurs. The abuser makes jokes about their behavior while still gaslighting you that it could have been worse: the classic questions in a sweet voice asking the survivor why they make the abuser act like that or why they cannot just understand, predict, and perfectly execute the abuser's needs. The Honeymoon phase is often farcical, a payment for the latter two phases. When you realize this phase is the payment, you might stop accepting it. That doesn't mean the abuser will stop taking what they believe they are owed in the form of abuse.

Recognizing the Honeymoon phase as the less genuine side of an abuser can help a person to develop a bad taste for the process like a bad artificial sweetener. This can lead to a desire to escape or not feed into the validation they so desperately seek during this phase. An abuser is also being rewarded here despite allowing you to feel indebted. They feel validated that they aren't that bad and their behavior is okay since you are still here. That doesn't mean they will react well if you plan to leave.

Leaving a toxic relationship is the most dangerous time in that relationship. It can automatically trigger an Explosive phase, as it validates the idea that they are not worth enough to stay with because of their bad behavior. In their codependent way, they will attempt to stop you from leaving to prove to themselves that they are not a bad person and not worthy of being alone. For this reason, abuse survivors tend to leave when the abuser is not home and will not catch them. The Honeymoon period is a common time to try and escape, as less attention is paid to the survivor's behavior and the bad actor is attempting to gain forgiveness/tolerance of their behavior.

The second phase in this cycle is the Tension Building or Frustration phase. Different diagrams will label it different things, but the cycle is the same. It is a period in which the abuser starts to nitpick and build toward a reason for a fight, although there may not be any reason when the phase begins. It is often related to their internal mood and regulation as to how they feel at that time. When an abuser feels bad, they will often seek a person on whom to release. In a relationship, that person is often the partner.

The Tension Building phase tends to be equivalent and correlated with the Honeymoon phase of this cycle. The longer an abuser lasts in the Honeymoon phase, the more they tend to pick apart behavior and issues in the Tension Building phase. This could be due to the disingenuous Honeymoon phase and the difficulty with which an abuser must maintain it. Malicious people cannot stay kind for lengthy periods of time and will often return to malicious behaviors like a rubber band. (The Rubber Band Theory was introduced by Dr. John Gray. However, he was discussing pulling away in relationships. Others have used this term to also describe the rubber band effect or regression to the mean effect of personality.)

A person cannot sustain not being themselves in a genuine way. This might be why politicians refuse to answer questions they would have to lie about while openly lying about many other things or why an abuser can appear to be such a good person in public and a monster at home. The Tension Building phase is the breaking down of the facade. The mimic can no longer hold their shape. This phase is the channeling of their negative energy, pain, and frustration into one person, commonly called the scapegoat.

Similar to the Honeymoon phase, the length of time the Tension Building phase lasts is correlated with the level of explosion in the Explosive phase. This can be why people in a scapegoat role might look as if they provoked the explosion. The longer the build of the tension, the easier and more reactive the release of that tension. The average person might ask, "Why would you provoke them?" to which a survivor would say, "I just wanted to get it over with," or something similar. The provocation is not the fault of the target of frustration. It is the natural conclusion to continuous and building pressure with the threat of release.

The average person who has not been in one of these relationships might be afraid during the process with the hope that it will end. The survivor of this cycle is just waiting for the abusive partner to pull the trigger, and when they don't, the target feels fed up with being threatened and will ask if they are going to. Resigning yourself to this cycle is not a good habit to end up in, but it is a place where survivors can find a sense of power. Being able to almost control the cycle can make it feel that much safer, even if from the outside looking in it looks consensual.

Active participation is not consent. Tolerance is not consent.

Channeling energy you have little control to stop is not consent. It is a form of fawning, as mentioned before. Placating a person who has power over you is not agreement to the abuse. It is survival. The movie *127 Hours* [17] is not about Ralston consenting to being trapped by a rock and patiently cutting off his arm to escape. In a similar vein, abuse is not always so one sided that the answer is to tolerate or not to tolerate. Financial abuse and social isolation are tools used in this Tension Building phase that stop survivors from leaving during or after the Explosive phase.

The Explosive phase is when the abuser can no longer hold in their pain and frustration, often having to do with themselves and an internal pain. They need someone to take it out on for a cathartic release. However, it is well known in the psychological community that catharsis is temporary relief. Breaking a plate in the kitchen feels good until you have no more plates and a mess to clean up. Catharsis is an ineffective coping strategy that tends to stack anger over time rather than resolve any of it.

The Explosive phase is the most dangerous time of the cycle. It can often lead to sexual assault as a means of taking back a perceived loss of power and is the phase when murder most often occurs in domestic violence. The Explosive phase is a complete release of any facade the abuser has been holding to appear normal. Everything internal will be projected outward, including self-hatred. This self-hatred is so explosive and painful, especially in the context of the next phase, that it can be confusing.

The average person does not tolerate being screamed at or yelled at and certainly should not tolerate being intimidated or threatened. However, this is a normal part of life for many survivors who have previously and still live in relationships of abuse. The usage of the emotional equity from the Honeymoon phase is traded in this phase, despite it not being a fair trade at all or really having any other choice. Anyone who has bought food or water at a theme park understands the abusive power dynamic and "trade-off" that happens in this phase at least to a minimal degree. $9 for water when you are parched might seem reasonable when otherwise you might laugh in the face of the person selling it, given other choices. The removal of these choices is the power.

It is difficult for the psyche to rationalize or understand how a person who at times can be so caring is acting like this and hurting you so much. Often the only explanation our minds can wrap around is that we must have done something to deserve this behavior. The truth of the matter is that no one deserves to be treated like this, no matter how good a person treats you at other times. The only reason we rationalize to ourselves as deserving the pain is that we can only understand our own thoughts in the context of our and others' behavior. If you truly knew the rationale for why a person chooses to harm you, you would never accept the behavior but would see it for how immature it truly is.

It is important to recognize when rationalizing during and after the Explosive phase, when you are in the Honeymoon phase, that if they wanted to they would. That is, if an abusive person wants to treat you like the king or queen, they convince you that they would not treat you as less than when their emotions were acting out. This is easiest to recognize if you are the scapegoat of the abuser. You are the target of their shifting behavior, and it is not normal even for them. Abusers cannot actively abuse everyone around them. They should be capable of not abusing you as well.

The niceness of the Honeymoon phase is confusing, as it seems like something you did in response to their unhappiness led to being treated correctly. This is nothing more than the experiment of the superstitious pigeon [18]. Skinner rewarded a pigeon randomly without specific cues to the reward. The pigeon developed ritualistic behavior and strange dances in a system that it believed would lead to reward. This is like the Explosive phase and the transition back into the Honeymoon phase. There is no reward; the chainsaw stopped because it ran out of gas. That is not something you must thank the chainsaw for.

The Honeymoon phase is even more toxic when you realize the emotional equity being developed through this process is mixed with the embezzlement of emotional equity by the abuser. The abuser takes two to every one coin of emotional equity banked, and they use this phase as a reward for tolerating their negative behavior during the Explosive phase while being validated for how well they treat you now. They also double dip this by publicly treating a survivor of abuse well and gaining even more validation from others. The abuser in this way is like a corrupt banker.

Chapter 6
Triangle of Trauma

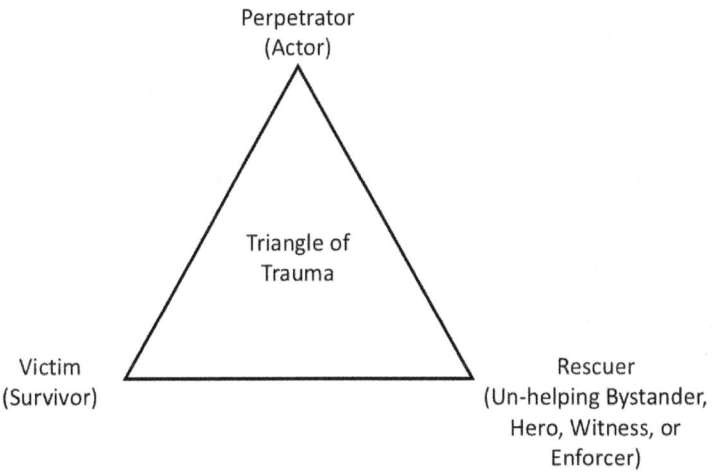

The triangle of trauma is a simple and yet complex mapping of the nature of relationships within a system of trauma that often makes it traumatic. The obvious positions on the triangle of trauma are the perpetrator and the victim. I believe most people would be able to identify those roles if asked to point them out. The more confusing position is often referred to as the rescuer. All these positions have multiple names, which I will try to explain in this chapter. However, the rescuer's role is less obvious because this triangle does not often end up with anyone being rescued.

The victim role is sometimes called the survivor, even if the person is still involved in the traumatic cycle. Every day they survive is a day they deserve the title of survivor. That is not to disparage anyone who has fallen victim to the process of trauma. Survivor is also a much easier title to be called than victim often is. The connotation to victim is a powerlessness that limits your ability to escape the process of abuse and remain a permanent fixture of this triangle. The victim role could also be called the target or receiver of abuse. Though, I feel like survivor might be the best option here.

As discussed in the previous chapter, through the cycle of abuse a survivor might act to provoke an explosion. We do not blame the victim for acting in a cycle of abuse that will lead to harm, no matter their behavior. This action is an attempt to gain a sort of control in a process in which they have none by design. Control often can feel like a form of safety. We don't blame people for wanting to feel safe when they are not causing harm to others or only acting in self-defense. However, the argument of self-defense is often weaponized by the abuser in that a person who clearly has more power than another claims they were defending themselves when the power dynamic alone was enough to prevent harm. We can see this in cases where abusers provoke an attack and seek a restraining order or a person with a gun claims self-defense against someone with a rock small enough to throw. They are not the same level of response and often beyond necessary use of force. We can refer to any behaviors by the survivor as seeking safety, like the trauma treatment approach that utilizes Cognitive Behavioral Therapy (CBT) to treat PTSD and Substance Use disorders.

A person without power is at the whim of those in control, and when a bad actor is in control, it is hard to label the person without power as anything other than a victim. A powerless person cannot just walk away, as walking away is a power move. Victims and survivors often seek some level of control in their lives when they are unable to control their safety. This can lead to the development of Obsessive-Compulsive disorder. The ritualistic behavior and magical thinking are a maladaptive form of control over a universe in which they have no control.

Radical acceptance is a way in which a person can accept a lack of control rather than try to create said control. It is an idea in mindfulness. In this universe the only control we have is to give up the illusion that we have any control at all and find safety in the acceptance of anything that happens. The rejection of truth is what causes much pain in the traumatic world. "That can't be true" or "I can't accept this" are common phrases by people who are traumatized. Never have I heard of a monk well practiced in acceptance report symptoms of trauma.

The suggestion of mindfulness and radical acceptance is not to shame any person that struggles with trauma. It is merely meant to offer a path. There are those who have Learned Helplessness, a term coined by Martin Seligman. He studied the effect on an animal when there was no available choice given to avoid pain. The animal would lay down and accept the coming pain following the signal. It might sound like radical acceptance, but Learned Helplessness continues and generalizes after the situation has changed. Learned Helplessness has hopelessness. Radical acceptance removes judgment and allows us to change when the situation changes. Learned Helplessness is much more pervasive and prevents us from attempting change. Seligman later focused on Positive Psychology, due to the emotionally challenging work in Learned Helplessness.

Learned Helplessness is a puzzling pattern to break. Breaking this pattern involves recognizing that there is something that can be done to avoid the pain and that you as the survivor can do this thing. How can a person survive so much pain and figure out a convoluted system of emotions with an emotionally immature caretaker or spouse and not be able to figure a way out of said pain? A strength-based model, which focuses on building and reinforcing the strengths already inherent in a person, has worked well in challenging this idea of hopelessness and helplessness when treating addiction. Active addicts wake up with no money in their pocket and often go to bed at the end of the day high with money in their pocket. Tell me that does not take strong attributes that if redirected would benefit them. Survivors are strong and often underestimate themselves.

The other obvious role in the triangle of trauma is that of the perpetrator. This role can also go by many names and will, depending on the role in the triangle receiving therapeutic treatment. They can be called the perpetrator, the abuser, or sometimes the actor or bad actor. We use the term actor when treating a person who might occupy this role in relationships. It is hard to want to change when the shame of being called a perpetrator is looming.

A bad person who wants to be good and stop doing bad things could be seen as a good person who needs help. This is a starting place for anyone trying to develop empathy for such people. They will not be helped without empathy to profoundly change, and that empathy can be exceedingly difficult to develop for some in cases that might trigger them. Even a therapist can be limited in their ability to hold empathy for a person, depending on how those issues interact with the therapist's own stuff. It takes a lot to see someone who caused intentional harm at one time and have emotional space for them, especially if you have ever been the target of similar harm. It is ethical for any person or therapist to not play the role of support for someone they struggle to look at without projecting guilt and shame. This can lead to relapse instead of recovery.

A place to start in developing empathy is remembering that abusers were often taught these behaviors through abuse inflicted on them. They go through a process in life where they learn to abuse others and take out their frustrations. The problem with anger linked to abuse is that it is often a feedback loop of maladaptive catharsis. As mentioned in the previous chapter about the use of catharsis for anger, the perpetrator's anger is similar in that it is not satisfied by abusing the victim. It tends to escalate due to the cathartic nature of the anger, depending on the harmful effect on the victim from a person who lacks empathy in that moment and cannot tell if their anger is being delivered except through physical or emotional exhaustion.

Anger is also a secondary emotion. This includes frustration, rage, and resentment or any other type of anger you can think of. It tends to cover pain, fear, or fear of being in pain. This is why all perpetrators were victims at some point in their life. It was the origin of the pain they then managed by developing the maladaptive coping skill of harming others. It is not for the victim or target of this pain to be the one who thinks they can heal it or save the perpetrator from it. You are the target for complex reasons that prohibit you from helping the perpetrator without triggering them further.

As in the case of the narcissist, the victim or target is often the person that reminds them most of themselves. Remember it is themselves that narcissists hate the most. It would be an insurmountable task to be the target or trigger of rage and the one who can soothe the anger. Even in the case of therapists, one who triggers a client to such a degree that it becomes unhealthy would do best to refer that person to another therapist.

The last role to discuss in this triangle of trauma is the role of the rescuer. The rescuer can also be known by many other titles. They can be called the rescuer, the hero, the witness, or even the un-helping bystander. This is the person who sees what is happening and either tries to help or not. The traumatic aspect of this role is the victim sees the role as a hope for help that is never quite able to remove them from the cycle of abuse. The triangle of trauma would not be traumatic if the victim could get away from the perpetrator and live a healthy life supported by the rescuer. Therein lies the fallacy of this triangle. The rescuer, even if they want to rescue, is unable to achieve this.

I tend to think of the scene in Home Alone when Kevin is in the grocery store buying himself groceries and the checkout person is asking him questions about who is taking care of him. Kevin, in this role and that time in the US, was taught not to let people know he was alone, whereas the person would have helped him be safe in that specific case. Sometimes the victim is taught not to ask for help with threats of worse harm, warnings that the outside world is much worse, or that people outside of the abusive system cannot be trusted.

Sometimes there are stories of a teacher or friend of the family who notices something is happening, as in the case of Drake Bell and his disclosure on *Quiet on Set* [19]. In some of these cases like Drake's, the rescuer is able to help and save the victim from the situation. However, it doesn't always happen this way. Sometimes the un-helping bystander is unhelping due to the perpetrator's ability to counteract their attempt to help.

Stories like this are told by survivors in this country where a person tried to help get the child out of harm's way, but the perpetrator was more trusted in the community and was able to alienate the rescuer. These cases are especially harmful due to the sudden hopelessness the victim must go through after believing they would be saved. This also tends to happen when the child reports a crime to an adult and the child is not believed or is even silenced.

The bystander effect also comes into play in these situations with the idea that *someone* will call the police to protect this child, so I don't have to. There are enough stories out there of women being attacked in broad daylight and no one doing anything about it. Mandated reporters exist to combat this issue, but it is not a perfect system and sometimes fails the children it is meant to protect. Articles discuss how survivors of sexual abuse placed in the foster system have then been abused by people in power of those systems. A Texas facility that cared for victims of sex trafficking were found to be sex trafficking those same kids [20]. There have also been examples of police taking a woman for a rape kit and raping her [21]. Or a priest meant to discipline a child for acting out on the bus using that opportunity to sexually abuse said child [22].

The triangle of trauma is complex and could shift, especially in family dynamics. The term triangulation can be used specifically in these instances where two of the roles team up against the other. The roles are also fluid and can change for each person through an argument, day, or relationship. A rescuer who rushes in to save the victim and beats up the perpetrator has just made the perpetrator into the victim. Sometimes this leads to the victim having to protect the perpetrator from the rescuer.

Other times, the victim takes the chance to swing back or throw something at the perpetrator out of frustration or in defense. This is the time when abusers will call the cops on their victims to initiate a protection from abuse order, more commonly known as a restraining order. Perpetrators can become the victim and use that position as one of power. The court system in our country allows this, especially in states that permit SLAPP suits (litigation designed as Strategic Lawsuits Against Public Participation). Think of all the cases where news networks or individual people are sued for defamation about something that was stated truthfully and thus not defamation. The goal is to make the financial cost of speaking out too great and to silence the truth through a form of DARVO.

The court system can play the role of the un-helping bystander in many cases. It is limited in its power to protect people without the proper evidence, and it is hard to collect evidence when you live with the person it would incriminate.

Family court is the best example of the un-helping bystander. Parents have rights to their kids, and the court cannot stop due process. Due process also doesn't happen quickly enough to prevent harm. It is also hard to know who to believe in any case when children could be manipulated by a parent. However, a manipulated kid looks just like a kid who rightfully does not like their parents for what has been done to them.

The role of rescuer or bystander is often not one that saves the victim or survivor. In this triangle, this role is utilized by the perpetrator to solidify the system and block the chance for escape. They can do this through overpowering the rescuer socially and creating distance where all the rescuer can do is watch and all the survivor can do is plead for help that will not come, and a level of hopelessness closes the door. Rescuers might even be part of a family system or social system that promotes keeping things calm and not provoking the perpetrator into more acts. The rescuer can also be a secondary perpetrator that reinforces the message that no one will treat the survivor better than the original perpetrator. This role of the rescuer may also be called the enforcer, which we will come back to later. It is often the interaction of these three positions that keeps the system in place and functioning in a harmful way.

Chapter 7
Posttraumatic Stress Disorder (PTSD)

PTSD is characterized by five primary criteria and a few criteria that are always included in each disorder in the Diagnostic and Statistical Manual Edition 5 (DSM) [23]. However, not all traumas would qualify for a diagnosis under the criteria of the DSM, since the DSM only manages disorders. A disorder is caused when the specific symptoms of said disorder inhibit life function in some way regarding work, school, social, or family life. Some of what is discussed in this chapter might strictly adhere to the most updated version of the DSM and some of it might only relate to it without meeting the threshold of criteria to be classified as disordered. A generic list of PTSD criteria are as follows. A-H are required. 1 and 2 signify specific presentations:

- A. Exposure
- B. Intrusive Symptoms
- C. Avoidance of Stimuli
- D. Negative Alteration in Cognition and Mood
- E. Increased Arousal Rating

Also included in the diagnostic criteria are:

- F. Symptoms last for more than one month

G. Symptoms create distress or functional impairment
H. Symptoms are not due to substances or another medical condition

There are two specifications or what were at one time labeled as qualifiers:

1. Dissociative specification
   a. Depersonalization: being an outside observer or detached from oneself (feeling like "this is not happening to me")
   b. Derealization: the feeling that the world is not real or is distorted
2. Delayed specification: the criteria of PTSD are not fully met until at least 6 months after the event/exposure [24]

Starting with the criterion that are not always present and not specifically the focus, the specifications are add-on symptoms/criteria if they are present in the individual presentation of PTSD. Dissociation is typically described as detaching or disconnecting from yourself or the world including thoughts, feelings, and emotions. Dissociation is also often mispronounced as dis-ah-sociation. There is no "ah" in the word, and it is pronounced dis-so-ciation. Dissociation is often described as spacing out or the thousand yard stare. It can also be described as on autopilot. There are two specific presentations of dissociation. You might feel like you are not you (depersonalization) or that the world is not real (derealization).

The other specification describes the diagnosis of PTSD as being met after six months from the onset of the exposure or events. This is not a requirement for the diagnosis of PTSD but rather a form of PTSD that can occur later and still be related to the original trauma. The criteria also describes that the onset of some symptoms can begin immediately following the event, but it does not have to and can't fully meet the criteria of diagnosis until six months later for this specification to be added.

The symptoms regarding duration (F), severity (G), and other explanations (H) are typical of most disorders in one way or another. Symptom F (requiring these symptoms for over a month) describes how they would be pervasive enough to not be temporary effects. This is similar to a depressive episode having to last at least two weeks. Many disorders have this time component. Symptom G is the symptom that determines something is disordered. A person who likes neat and clean things might note that they have OCD. However, unless the symptoms disrupt their life in a way described by symptom G, they might be obsessive or compulsive without the disorder. Symptom H is our catch-all. Substance-induced symptoms or general medical conditions causing an issue must be eliminated before any disorder can be ascribed.

The five primary criteria of PTSD start with exposure. This might seem obvious, but for something to be posttraumatic then something traumatic must first happen. It is the witnessing of the event or exposure to this event that meets this criterion. The exposure can also be secondary, as in learning that the traumatic event happened to someone close to you or having a traumatic exposure event described to you, often in enough detail to affect you. The secondary version is often referred to as vicarious traumatization and is why in group settings the details are often left vague. I have heard therapists say vicarious traumatization is what stops them from being able to treat trauma specifically. And no, a therapist is not supposed to be able to treat anything and everything under the sun. We need to know we can keep our stuff out of your stuff to avoid countertransference. Transference is the projection of emotions toward others in a person's life onto the therapist, and the therapist doing the same response in return is countertransference.

The second criterion refers to what I labeled as intrusive symptoms. This means that aspects of the trauma are repeatedly experienced after the event has ended. This can include physical symptoms like freezing or suddenly having the urge to run or fight. It can involve reactivation of the emotions that happened during the exposure. There can also be nightmares, memories, and flashbacks to the exposure event. The intrusive aspect of these symptoms is that they are happening despite a desire for them not to happen and are persisting to a point where they are distressing.

Flashbacks and memories are different from each other. Most people know what a memory is to a degree. Memories come in two forms. There is explicit or recall memory that often is seen as a picture or movie in our head, excluding those with aphantasia, who have a limited ability to imagine pictures in the mind. When I ask you to imagine a red apple, what do you see in your mind? If nothing, talk to someone about aphantasia.

Implicit memory is the physical sensation that is a replication of how you felt at the time of the event, even if there is no recall memory associated. For example, this may be due to the memory forming before recall memory was available (around the age of three).

Flashbacks are the physical experience of what would seem to be a memory, but it is remembered and felt as if it is happening in the present. A recent study showed that memory is stored in the back of our head and brought forward while flashbacks or traumatic memories are stored in the front and brought back in the same way that memory is formed [25].

The third criterion is the avoidance of stimuli, specifically stimuli related to the trauma that triggers intrusive symptoms or reminds a person of the experience and which a person desires to avoid, to such a degree it becomes maladaptive. Driving around town to avoid a spot that increases a trip from a few blocks would be considered avoidance of stimuli. A stimulus can also generalize. We see this in the experiment of little Albert, where he was startled with a loud noise to make him afraid of rats while they were present but this fear generalized to anything white and fluffy. The experimenters, Watson and Rayner, would not be able to ethically replicate this study in the same way today.

The fourth criterion to the diagnosis of PTSD is negative alteration in cognition and mood. The easiest way to understand that complicated sentence is that the trauma started a process of thinking poorly and feeling poorly about yourself or the world following the event. "Negative" also means removing something, as memories can be lost due to this criterion. These memories and feelings that are experienced are also overly negative compared to how an average person might feel. In other words, it is thinking or feeling so poorly that you are unable to get out of bed or go to work, and it cannot be attributed better to depression or anxiety.

The fifth criterion of PTSD is known as increased arousal rating. Arousal in the terms of psychology and in the context of PTSD relates to the fight or flight response or the response of the body to life-or-death situations. In PTSD, the arousal increase is trauma-related and can also affect reactivity if these changes came after the trauma. The increase in this rating and reactivity means a decrease in the required amount of triggering material to push a person into this state. Simply put, a person with an increased arousal rating will enter the fight or flight state much faster and easier than their baseline before the trauma. This can appear as irritability or anger, destructive behavior, hypervigilance, being easily startled, and having difficulty with concentration and/or sleep.

So, what does all this mean for a person who has PTSD or has experienced trauma in their life? In short it means that something bad enough happened to them that they don't want to be reminded of it happening, despite the symptoms intruding on their life and making them feel badly about themselves while also being hyperaware that it could happen again. A person fearful of being harmed can start to see harm in other areas of the world and react to them despite those generalized fears not exactly matching the original trauma.

How does PTSD affect a person's life? Well, it depends. That will be your most common answer due to the myriad of presentations of symptoms. In general, it can cause a person to be less trusting, more alert, and avoidant of people, places, and things that might hurt them whether that belief is realistic. Isolation and emotional pain, a loss of control over one's own body, and even complete disconnection from reality are all possible. However, the funny thing about these debilitating symptoms is they are designed for survival, and in cases where that is not possible, relief from the process of death. You don't want to feel the process of being eaten alive, so the brain numbs these signals, similar to other times your brain thinks you are dying.

Why is PTSD so crippling? When the mind is not forced to focus on survival every moment of every day, we can create and explore the world. However, when we are not guaranteed survival or at least given the illusion of that guarantee, it is incredibly difficult to focus on anything else. Depictions in popular media show characters as more animalistic in this phase, like Robin Williams as Alan Parish in *Jumanji* or Drizzt as the hunter in survival mode from R.A. Salvatore's extensive series starting in the *Dark Elf Trilogy*.

Does PTSD ever go away? It can. At the very least the symptoms can be reduced if they don't go into full remission. In therapy we discuss the process of no longer having to survive but getting to live or thrive. This means being able to move past the nonacceptance of the trauma and develop a life in accepting all of you from day one through now. Rejection of any part of you is rejection of *you*. That doesn't often lead to a lot of healing.

Acceptance is often the path to healing. Acceptance and safety lead to a better outcome.

It can be difficult to live with a person who has PTSD. Triggering events can lead to tense confrontations in which a person views a situation as life or death when a plate breaks in the kitchen and everything is okay. The way in which traumatic memory is stored links current events to past traumatic reactions. So, a traumatic response to loud noises or making messes in the past can surface in the current moment. A good support for someone with PTSD is to affirm that everything is okay, and everyone is safe in the here and now.

PTSD is a serious mental illness that should be treated with respect. It is not as dangerous as often portrayed in the media. However, not everyone is prepared to handle strong triggers from trauma. The best thing can be to remain calm, stay safe, and talk about how the person wants to be reacted to outside of the crisis. A de-escalation trainer once told me, "You are less likely to be punched in the face if they have a rapport with you." I have found this to be true in de-escalation . . . even when it was close to not being true.

Chapter 8
PTSD Symptoms and Avoidance

Many of the symptoms related to PTSD have the direct goal of avoidance. Trauma is not something people often run toward but something people tend to run from. Avoidance of stimuli is not the only symptom of trauma in which people are actively avoiding the reminders or triggers of said trauma, though it is certainly a main contributor. One might argue—and I plan to—that every symptom of trauma outside of exposure is related to the avoidance of what was traumatically exposed. From the moment of exposure, the mind tries to protect itself with avoidance.

The state in which people are often found following a severe trauma is a state of dissociation. The person's mind, to protect them, has severed ties to memory, emotion, and thought. They don't feel like themselves, or they feel like nothing is real. This is an attempt by the brain to distance them from that painful realization of the trauma, the realization they are not safe. Following air, food, water, and shelter needs being met, safety is the next need. When the world is unsafe, maladaptive safety can be found in denial.

Though our brain severed the connection, it does not seem to have an ability to automatically reconnect or even have an open line of communication with us following trauma. It will send us glimpses and emotions based on triggers to see if we are ready to process what has happened. The intrusiveness of this process grows stronger as a person attempts to resist and avoid. The brain may start with reminders and move into stronger stimuli when ignored. Nightmares and flashbacks are usually the worst of the intrusions.

So, a person does what any human would do and tries to avoid the pain while sometimes seeking pleasure. The traumatized person may go out of their way to avoid stimuli that remind them of the trauma in any way. They could drive longer distances around triggers, start missing days of school or work, become isolated from their social network, or many other things that can harm them in the long run. Temporary avoidance can be fine and even a good thing. However, it takes on a maladaptive context when it starts to inhibit a person's ability to return to their baseline or normal behavior.

The negative alterations can also be a form of avoidance. The lack of access to memories of the incident is a clear form of avoidance being handled by your brain. Having negative thoughts about yourself or the world and exaggerating blame can be a way in which a person seeks to feel they have some kind of control in life, even if it means believing they caused the issue. Losing interest in things you once enjoyed and feeling isolated or different from others is further avoidance. The term for this feeling of isolation is "terminally unique": using the belief that no one can understand your pain as a way of isolating.

Oddly enough, increased arousal rating is also a form of avoidance. The fight, flight, freeze, or fawn state is an attempt to avoid something. Irritation and aggression are forms of the fight response. A heightened startle response is a form of the flight response, along with the urge to be somewhere else. Boredom falls into this category of flight response/avoidance, which I will attempt to address in a later chapter on ADHD. Hypervigilance is an early and continuous part of the freeze response. Destructive behavior, hypervigilance, and difficulty sleeping and concentrating are also parts of both the freeze and fawn response. These symptoms of PTSD are intricately connected to avoidant behavior.

At first, the process of avoidance in the traumatic response is to protect the individual. The issue is when this response lasts for a long time, so that the incident becomes so powerful that it will leak into every aspect of a person's life. The people we become after our trauma cannot be accepted without first accepting the events that led to it. The wounded version of ourselves that was introduced to the trauma needs to be cared for, and we can't do that blindfolded. Wounds that are ignored will fester.

This festering is why avoidance makes PTSD worse. Fear of rejection or public humiliation will follow a person until they can properly process the event that led to that harm. Healing is often intermingled with self-care. While self-care as a concept is well-known, it is often misunderstood or misused. In reality, it is a fancy buzzword for self-soothing. When we are hurt as children, we are supposed to be soothed by someone so that we can learn to soothe ourselves. Self-care is that attempt to soothe ourselves. Avoidance is the opposite, something that some people have had in their life: neglect.

Neglect is a fitting example of avoidance. Why would a person neglect someone or something? Perhaps looking at that person reminds them of their inadequacies in life. Perhaps taking care of something forces you to look at it even if it has bad memories attached. Because of this, we often hide away things and memories, so we don't have to be reminded. If you hide poison by swallowing it, it might hurt you, or worse. Avoidance is just that. It has been said resentment is like swallowing poison and hoping the other person dies. Resentment too is a form of avoidant emotion.

How can you stop avoidance from PTSD? A good start is with vulnerability, opening to people, and building a support system you can be vulnerable with. Start small. Vulnerability is scary since it leaves us open to being further wounded. However, it can be our chance to show those around us the parts of ourselves that we struggle to accept. Having others help us model acceptance of our vulnerabilities can be an immense help. It can also strengthen healthy relationships. Besides that, vulnerability often encourages more vulnerability and can deepen the bonds and trust in your support system.

Even though vulnerability can be scary, when the people we are vulnerable to choose not to wound us, we gain trust and emotional strength. Vulnerability is the opposite of avoidance. It is embracing the defects or feared pain. When we are vulnerable, we remove the ability for shame to grow as we bring our fears and pain into the light to heal.

Like I said, start off small to build trust with those around you. Ease into the process. Too fast, and the shame and guilt can overtake you and make it so you may avoid these people in the future. That is why I often encourage people not to bare it all in the first session when it comes to trauma. They tend not to come back if they do.

The urge to avoid is just that: the urge to not come back. We often think we have more control over ourselves than we are aware. The problem with having control is that you need to understand all that is happening at any given time. However, this area of urges is not completely understood as language in our brain; instead, it is like an arrow that points in a direction, and we are driven to travel for some magical thing to satiate our need. Urges are not so mysterious once you understand their origin, and I have an idea on how they might work.

As we have explicit and implicit memory, we also have explicit and implicit language. The explicit is in our own voice in our head and speaks in our native tongue. It is easy to understand. However, implicit language comes from the body even if it is put there by the brain. We understand the explicit language to come from our prefrontal cortex or executive functioning area of the brain. This is where rationale and logic are located. Implicit language comes from the limbic system, an area that developed earlier in our evolution than the prefrontal cortex.

It may be easier to picture the prefrontal cortex like the adult in our brain, as it typically finishes developing last in our adulthoods. The limbic system could more easily be imagined as the inner child of our brain. It is the reactive part of us that is often harder to soothe. Our logical mind can try to interpret the emotional mind if you are aware of how the emotional mind speaks. I worked in the world of addiction for ten years and found the mind in active addiction and early recovery is often controlled by this emotional mind.

This is why relapse happens and people trying to remain in recovery struggle to know why. Many users of downers report trying to escape the pain, while users of stimulants often report just wanting to have fun. Rationally, why aren't they having fun without the substances? They may not be aware of the implicit language in their body screaming for comfort. Substance users are often avoiding something, whether it is through downers to numb or stimulants to escape themselves. We will return to substance use in a later chapter.

So, if we treat this emotional mind as our inner child and use our rational mind to take care of its needs, then we might not feel the urge to escape. Boredom would not exist if this voice was taken care of. You know this if even one time in your life you have been sitting in a room not doing something and not felt bored. Boredom is the urge to escape, move, change, etc. People tell me that it helps to think about their emotional mind as their inner child who they want to protect and comfort. This is a good approach, and we have not seen negative side effects from caring for ourselves.

Again, this is self-care. Caring for our emotions or inner child and their emotional needs for comfort and soothing is an especially important thing we can do. When our emotional mind is taken care of, we seem to focus better and sit still longer. Urges are the screams of desperation from our inner child. When we don't listen to them, we end up engaging in self-destructive behaviors with food, spending, sex, or drugs. Our inner child craves dopamine for soothing. We can also achieve this through curiosity, doing things that motivate us, and engaging in things that excite us.

Part III: Complex Trauma

Chapter 9
Complex PTSD

The "C" in CPTSD is meant to specify the extent and type of trauma that might have been endured. Complex trauma is often complex because the survivors of it will take responsibility for their trauma and often protect the perpetrator or actor due to the nature of how these traumas are formed. The complexity comes from a trauma formed in a relationship that has an extreme power differential (an imbalance in control) in which one person often relies on another, and care is at risk if the survivor were to point out the pain.

The National Health Service (NHS) of the United Kingdom describes common symptoms of CPTSD as difficulty managing emotions or having/maintaining relationships. It also lists shame, guilt, worthlessness, emotion regulation difficulty, struggles with connectedness, and relationship instability [26]. The CPTSD foundation identifies the ongoing and unavoidable nature of CPTSD [27]. It properly notes this type of trauma is the result of a relationship with another person where said person affects the survivor's ability to maintain emotional safety.

CPTSD is a result of trauma, but it is the result in a specific way. The trauma causes more of the freeze or fawning response rather than the fight or flight response. These are the responses a person will use where there is no escape and the power differential is too much. Often, a survivor of this type of trauma is dependent on a caretaker who is abusive or neglectful. This is not always the case, as it could be due to a teacher, bully, boss, or other individual with power over the survivor. The primary aspect is a relationship that depends on trust, and that trust leads to harm, repeatedly.

We see questions in the media like, "Why don't you just leave?" There was even a hashtag movement in 2014 known as #WhyIStayed [28]. The answer is not a simple one due to an aspect of trauma that many struggle to conceptualize: time. These relationships are culminations of smaller traumas (little t's) with some typical traumas (big T's) along the way causing the trauma. However, it is not all at once, and often the abusive person knows how far to push before pulling back. But make no mistake: A person who pushes a boundary and backs up is only building up speed to crash through it.

You have had this experience, and you have not. Imagine with me a time when you might have been planning to go out into the cold or rain for a long time and you thought what you were wearing would be enough to protect you. After arriving at the event or some time into it, the wind cuts through you or the rain starts to soak in rather than bead off. You could go home, but is it really that bad? You chose to wear this anyway. You can tough it out. Time after time the wind or rain wears away your body heat to the point where you can start to feel that chill at your core temperature. The one that is hard to come back from. You could go home and change, but people around you encourage you to stay, and you hope that if you stay everything will be worth it in the end.

Hours go by. Your toes and fingers are numb. You can't protect yourself against the elements anymore. You start to think this is *your* fault for not being prepared. You don't want to ruin everyone else's fun by leaving early. It is at this point in the relationship that the abusive person attacks by staying longer, affirming fears of fault, or using the word "weak" when you have nothing left and would be dependent on them to survive. This moment will be drawn on for years as to why you cannot leave. They saved you. However, this way of thinking is flawed since it draws on earlier lessons of self-worth and other relationships.

Survivors are told that no one else would treat them as kindly as the abuser and that this was all a favor, or they felt sad for you. Children can even be told about some of the ugly truths of the foster system if they threaten to call the authorities. Many women and children are not believed, and fewer men still report the abuse. Society does not want to believe this harm is happening every day behind closed doors.

Which leads to another issue I have found in treating people with CPTSD. Family, friends, and society often do not believe a person is capable of the things that are said and done behind these closed doors. Other times, the specific instances of abuse seem mundane to the average person due to them not having the same pain points or triggers as the survivors that are targets repeatedly. Survivors are often invalidated, even by people who love them. Healthy relationships will sometimes question the validity with, "Are you sure?" or "I can't believe they would say/do something like that!"

Perhaps you can understand my analogous story above and relate to it. You think it seems silly how a person would allow themselves to be harmed to such a degree. If you are the latter, be careful how you speak to survivors. Only they know what they have been through. Invalidation makes problems quiet. It does not fix them. Survivors of CPTSD have enough trouble opening up about their abuse in the first place, often fearing they are the "bad guy" or they themselves believing they must be blowing it out of proportion. They don't need help gaslighting themselves.

Having CPTSD often makes you feel like you just can't get anything right, people come and go and abandon you, there is no one to trust, and the fear of being to blame for not leaving is enough to never say anything. CPTSD can be detected in many ways. The way that I tend to first notice it is when a person is describing themselves as not being able to get anything right or not having value. I tend to ask where they learned that they are worthless in this belief system. Sometimes I ask if someone spoke to them that way or might have been highly critical.

Survivors often note the highly critical person. This person tends to be an authority figure in their life. They then suddenly can switch to defending these actions by noting the worthlessness this person sees as valid and needing correction. We are not born hating ourselves. We are taught to do so. We are often taught through the projection of the shortcomings of a caretaker or someone we come to trust. That is why it hurts so much and is believed with such vigor. Someone who loves you would never say anything to hurt you, right?

Why is CPTSD so hard to treat? It's cognitive distortion. It's the belief as an individual that you were a failure in some way and that if only you could have been good enough at that one thing, you would be able to be loved. This is what is called a false epiphany. No relationship is solved by being the best at just one thing. I saw it in addiction treatment centers all the time. "I just have to . . ." The key in that sentence is "just." If it were that easy, you would have solved it. You are capable, but the problem is bigger.

This idea of trading the skill that you are supposed to excel at for love is absolutely a form of transactional love. This is the opposite of unconditional love. It's also a false form of love, as it depends on what you can do for someone else. Unhealthy authority figures who love only when you are good enough do not actually love. It is far worse than love or not love. Survivors of CPTSD are often attempting to be "good enough" to be loved. Or so they think.

The truth of transactional love is that we are not seeking to be good enough to be loved. We are seeking to be good enough to not be abused. In the mind of a survivor, these are often seen as the same thing. However, stating it the latter way is far less desirable a goal. No person should have to prove that they don't deserve to be abused. No one deserves abuse. That statement might trigger some, but think about it. Would the abuser abuse if they themselves had not been abused and taught to abuse?

That is not to say that we allow people to abuse us or others. It's best to keep people at a distance where they are no longer able to abuse you when possible. This is the idea of going no contact that I will discuss later in the boundaries chapter. We must believe others when they speak out and distance ourselves from the reach of harm of potential abusers.

So far, we have discussed narcissism and trauma to a great extent. This section is meant to discuss the furtherance of said trauma that can happen in relationships and often happens in a relationship with a narcissistic or highly critical person. These feelings of worthlessness and self-doubt are amplified if not also implanted in the mind of a person through the importance of the relationship. They tend to create an internal monologue in our own voice that will use the words of this highly critical person. The voice is amplified and affects us in a negative way.

The movie *Inception* [29] was inaccurate. It is amazingly easy to implant ideas in a person's head. Think about a time you were talking about tacos, and someone later produced the idea of tacos for dinner. Think of a time you introduced something to your family only to be ignored and three months later a different family member is exaggerating that thing. In the psychology of learning, this is called priming. It is pointing at the thing you want people to notice for later. It increases salience or prominence.

Now imagine that there is a voice in your head that is more critical than normal and speaks in the same voice as *you*, since there is not exactly sound in your head's monologue. You have been primed through a complex and traumatic relationship to notice all your faults. You may even forget about these phrases that are often repeated and have been learned from someone else. You might start to think they are your own. Your head is no longer a safe place for you to exist, but you cannot escape.

Chapter 10
The Effect of Stress on Focus and Concentration

Anyone who has ever felt stress in the process of trying to complete a task will know that mistakes are made that seem silly and should have been avoided. I often think of the scene from *Rocket Man* (1997) in which the main character is expected to rewire a panel while being spun in all different directions in a gyroscope. It was meant to simulate trying to do this task at the worst possible moment. Through much of the movie, the task seems impossible due to the stress.

Stress is a complex thing, and through this chapter we will be referring to perceived stress as simply "stress," as it is the subjective experience of stress by an individual rather than general stress. Similar to trauma, where something might be traumatic to one person but not be traumatic to the next, something might be more stressful to one person and not be as stressful to another. Here we are not determining the stressors but rather their effects.

Our brains have limitations. As we approach those limitations, it can be perceived as stress. Stress might be a form of limiting stimuli created in our bodies as a reaction to a demanding situation to help us understand our limitations and not to push past them for the safety of our body. However, we don't always have this level of control. That's especially true in the context of a power dynamic differential. Stress is a limiter that we cannot shut off, but we can try to push through. Pushing through these limiters can cause damage over a long time and lead to them acting earlier and more frequently.

The fight or flight response of the body entering survival mode is the stress discussed in this context. The more often this process is activated, the easier it is that this process will be activated in the future. The fight or flight response is not normally triggered in the average population on even a yearly basis, whereas it can be a daily occurrence for someone who is consistently exposed to this level of traumatic and perceived stress. The more often it activates, the more it becomes an automatic response, and the less control a person has over it.

People living in a situation in which they have little to no control can't always avoid this triggering, and the automatic responses of freeze and fawn become increasingly common with each triggering event. A voice in the head of a person who cannot control or command said voice to stop or pause the negativity is absolutely under these levels of stress. See, the sneaky part of emotional abuse is the ability for the abuser to replicate themselves inside of someone else's head. This provides 24/7 torment with less effort required.

The fight or flight response is like those switches you see in movies that are typically covered by a red, plastic covering and often meant to launch missiles. The switch is fine when used in emergencies sometimes. Some people never have to flip said switch. However, imagine with me if you will, a person who must flip the switch so often that they rarely ever leave arm's reach of said switch. That switch might start to get a little flimsy. The red plastic cover has broken off over the years. One day the switch breaks in the "on" position. The more often a person enters the fight or flight response, the easier it becomes to enter a state that is meant for life-or-death situations, to the point it may become automatic. This is a stress response, or rather the response *to* the stress response. It becomes more stressful until at least dissociation, but that is a different matter.

Can you imagine coming home to do homework in the living room or at the kitchen table while being surrounded by chaos, or even worse, being the target of said chaos? 2+2 no longer equals 4 in those moments. 2+2 might start to equal "is it 2, two, too, or to? Who created numbers and who started the process of adding them together? What is added? Are numbers all the same in every language? I had a two-dollar bill once." The mind is desperately seeking to be anywhere else. It is seeking safety. This is not a distraction out of a lack of discipline. This *is* discipline, to feel safe in chaos. I bet if danger appeared or someone called their name, this person would react immediately despite being "distracted."

I'll give another example of the application of pressure or stress on a simple thing. Imagine signing your name. Easy, right? Now imagine someone pushing down on your hand as you are signing said name. The signature might start to be affected by the stress of the outside force, impacting your handwriting.

Wait. People with ADHD are often known for bad handwriting. That's not a good example.

Imagine riding in the car. Have you ever tried to write in a car? There is a slight jostle to the movement of the car that prevents the ability to write smoothly. You can't stop the movement, and it affects your writing.

I've strayed too far from the point. Take it from this study. "Chronic stress overloads the attention system, thereby reducing the amount of attention resources available to allocate to less relevant information" [30]. Liu et al. also discuss the consequences of prolonged exposure, such as an increased vulnerability to psychological, cognitive, and physical illnesses [30]. This study relates the impact on attention control to these stressors. We have seen how the development of the limbic system is affected by stressors along with the lack of attention or focus to specific stimuli.

The scene of saving a person who has been stressed or even tortured for lengthy periods of time often depicts a person as in a state that can't calm down or even look someone in the eyes to focus on what they are saying until some sort of soothing takes place. This is not unlike real life. The first rule of crisis response is to remove the trigger if possible. Then provide a safe space for the person to calm down while providing that calm emotional anchor for them. Their breathing starts to slow, and their eye movements become more intentional. After a time, the person can see and hear you. They will even be able to have a conversation, despite having been in a state of pure panic. This soothing is difficult for people with complex trauma.

Complex trauma is not just CPTSD either. It is the formation of multiple and separate diagnoses in the DSM. Many disorders come from stress, and these results are even more likely if the stress continues for a long period of time [31]. Some of the disorders that can develop due to complex trauma include: Reactive Attachment Disorder, Dissociative Identity Disorder, Dissociative disorders, Eating disorders, Anxiety disorders, Panic disorders, Phobias, Obsessive Compulsive Disorder, Somatic disorders, Sleep-wake disorders, Personality disorders, Disruptive/Impulse control/Conduct disorders, Sleep disorders, Paraphilias, Sexual dysfunctions, Substance Use disorders, and, *I* believe, specifically ADHD.

The inverse effect of stress also has merit to it. An 85-year longitudinal study known as the Grant Study investigated what makes us happy in life and tracked the death of people in the study to see the differences. This study found that the largest effect on our longevity and what makes us happier over our life to reduce stress were positive relationships [32]. Healthy and positive relationships are a core coping skill any therapist is going to ask about (your support system). People who have a support system that they don't feel shame from can go home after something bad happens and talk about it.

Trauma is often stressful and traumatic due to the survivor feeling like they must fix the problem themselves or survive it alone. The perpetrator adds to this belief through shame and social isolation. People who go home after a trauma and tell their support system and are validated don't tend to end up in my office. The traumatic part of these issues is having to face them alone with the shame and guilt of believing that you somehow caused it. There is no amount of anything in this world that would be consent for others to harm you to a point you feel like you can never tell anyone or face loved ones again.

Does stress affect your ability to focus? Absolutely! There is something called the Stress Response Curve that shows this effect in sports psychology. As stress and arousal increase, many people's performance will also increase. At a high point on the curve, the arousal can become too much and starts to inhibit the performance of a player. Think of a case of nerves, the yips, or a player who often chokes when the game is on the line. This would be an example of the choke point/drop off. This limit is different for everyone, but it does exist.

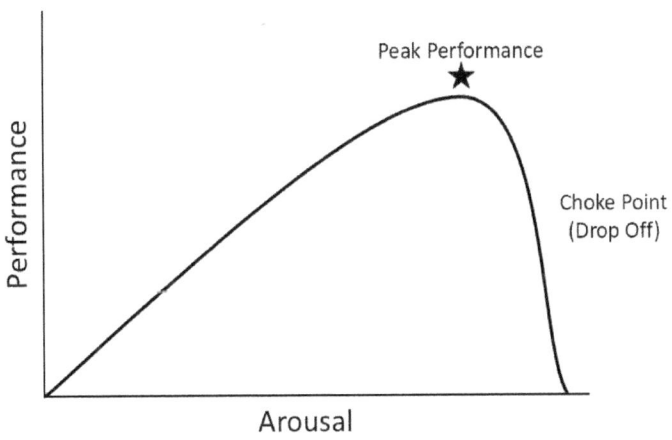

Heir of Narcissism

    This example also works for what we might call "gifted kid anxiety," where a child is praised for their intelligence and begins to think the only meaning they have is their brain and ability to understand complex concepts and to be successful. I tend to run into two types of gifted kids later in life. I have met with people who have horrible anxiety due to never having failed yet and are barely keeping it together, and I have met those gifted kids who have fallen from the pedestal and are terrified to get back up to fail again. The first is working past the peak of their performance, and the latter has fallen down the slope after failure and exhaustion.

    One last example of how stress can affect concentration and focus has to do with eyewitnesses. They are notoriously bad at identifying details after a stressful event because trauma and stress can affect the memory process while also affecting what's focused on. Some testimony might only note the color of the gun and vehicle while others can get clothing, height, and hair. Ask ten different people at a crime scene what they saw, and you will get ten different answers. This stress fogs the brain. The best way to rewire the brain to have better recall, focus, and concentration is to develop a sense of safety.

Chapter 11
ADHD

ADHD feels like more of a misnomer than anything else in the diagnostic realm of psychology. People with ADHD don't have deficits in attention as much as they have interest in subjects, and I know that sounds like I am just splitting hairs. Realistically it comes down to dopamine and the mechanisms in the brain around dopamine. Dr. Gabor Maté describes dopamine as the chemical in the brain that allows and promotes curiosity, vitality, and motivation [33]. These are the areas that promote or inhibit attention in anything. I would say most people have to care about something to focus on it, it must give them a sense of purpose to follow through on, and we must have the desire to focus on it.

ADHD is not a deficit in the ability to pay attention. It is more of a deficit in the ability to pay attention to things we don't care about. *Futurama* has an episode titled "Obsoletely Fabulous" where we meet a robot that runs off water power and must run into the ocean every time her water runs out [34]. Similar to ADHD, asking her to go to the grocery store away from said water would be a no-go. However, if she learned her purpose in life and understood something more profound, but would have to travel through the desert to get there with the risk of not making it, she might work hard to try. This is what seems to not make sense to neurotypical understanding of ADHD. It is not a deficit of attention; it is a deficit of motivation.

Hyperactivity is also a strange aspect to the name of this disorder. Many of the parts that are labeled hyperactive feel more appropriate to call "uncomfortable in neurotypical situations," combined with impulse control issues in distress tolerance. We could almost combine those two to mean a version of distress tolerance. ADHD could better be viewed through the lens of sensory processing issues rather than attention and hyperactivity. The "A" and "H" in the disorder name are more symptoms of the overarching issue related to sensory processing.

The criteria in the inattentive section of ADHD from the DSM, "Often does not seem to listen when spoken to directly," is absolutely a depiction of the underlying auditory processing issue. It would better be explained by noting the common "what?" followed by an answer to the question they heard but needed more time to process. The other issue this criterion does not consider is a neurotypical person not ensuring the neurodivergent person wasn't already occupied. I can't tell you how many times people will start talking to me while I'm focused on something else and get mad when I don't hear what they said. There's a reason you're not supposed to talk in the movies, and that rule was not made to accommodate neurodivergent people.

If we were to go through all the criteria for a diagnosis of ADHD, it would be clear that the symptoms that meet these criteria are more attached to sensory processing. What is sensory processing in the context of ADHD? Well, sometimes we need to be stimulated and other times we are over stimulated. It is the dysregulation of stimulation that often leads to sensory processing issues.

How can it be both? I used to think that people with ADHD were either/or. I have noticed since being diagnosed that it depends on the circumstances. I don't want to be alone in my own head all the time with my thoughts running wild and sometimes will utilize distraction to limit my brain's ability to run. Other times, I want to focus on something and am having trouble not paying attention to everything around me and will prefer to isolate my brain to focus.

The ADHD brain is like a microphone. It can focus on a specific sound, or it can hear everything around it. This can be good and bad, depending on the goal of the person using the microphone. Society loves our ability to act in a crisis, but they hate our difficulty sitting still in an office cubicle. A microphone that picks up everything is too sensitive for most jobs. A microphone that picks up only one specific thing is not sensitive enough. This is like the disordered abilities of a person with ADHD. They can be too specialized for daily use.

Typical symptoms that are not specifically listed in the criteria for ADHD are:

Symptom	Issue
Sensory Issues	Cognitive Processing
Avoiding Eye Contact	Rejection/Avoiding Fawn Response
Emotion Regulation	Shame/Guilt/Lack of Boundaries
Executive Function	Distress tolerance/Inhibition Control
Social Difficulties	Hearing/Organizing/Communicating
Bottom-Up Thinking	Need to Understand First
Insomnia	Alone in Thought/No Distraction
Rejection Sensitivity	Fear of Abandonment/Not Good Enough
Clumsiness	Distracted by Thought or Intention
Demand Avoidance	Lack Safety/Control

These symptoms are left out of the criteria for the disorder, and yet they seem present in many people with ADHD. The theme of these symptoms is a desire to feel safe and in control of oneself and surroundings without the fear of abandonment or self-deprecation. It's funny how focusing on the attention, hyperactivity, and cognitive processing ideas these disorders have overlook the true issue. The brain does not feel safe, and it is difficult to control to make it feel safe. Coping skills are hard to maintain and manage due to issues with habit formation, and the fear of loss of a support system is a regular occurrence in relation to the emotional dysregulation that can end relationships quickly.

I see a person with ADHD as someone who struggles with trying to do too much and an inability to tolerate doing too little. They often want to be accepted and loved, feel safe, and meet the needs of others around them without fear of abandonment. The disordered aspect of this diagnosis is more closely related to the attempt to fit into a society that is not made to accept them. A person with ADHD absolutely can live a normal life, given the right coping skills and support system.

Many of us were not diagnosed until after the 2020 lockdown, which limited coping skills and brought out the negative symptoms to a noticeable level. ADHD got worse without treatment to the point many people sought treatment for the first time during the lockdown. Your brain tells you that you just need energy to be able to function again and promotes rest and relaxation, but these lead to depleted energy, as rest does not promote dopamine production or use. Life can be hard with ADHD. The symptoms can be frustrating for other people and yourself. The dysregulation can cause blow-ups that damage relationships. Living with ADHD can be hard, and the pandemic made us aware of that, since ADHD also often numbs the negative symptoms.

One of the dark sides of ADHD is fawning behavior in relationships. The person with ADHD will create a mask that they think others will like more than themselves and overstep their own boundaries to please them. This is an exhausting process and a recreation of the trauma from childhood. It can only be tolerable for so long before the mask becomes too exhausting and the emotions start to build. People with ADHD after months or years of hiding their needs will suddenly burst with raw emotion in what some call an emergent need.

This sudden explosion of emotion would catch most people off guard. Healthy people tend to distance themselves from this type of behavior. The people we are left with who will tolerate this explosion of emotion are not typically healthy themselves. A *Just for Today* [35] meditation for April 1st says this: "We made impossible demands, driving away those who had anything of worth to offer us. Often, the only people left were those who were themselves too needy to be capable of denying our unrealistic expectations." This often leads to abandonment that we had created in the withholding of our true selves.

The self-fulfilling prophecy of abandonment recreates itself repeatedly until healthier behaviors are adopted. This abandonment and desperate need to avoid it happening are often the *cause* of the abandonment in the end. Attention and focus are one thing, but people with ADHD struggle with relationships. I will discuss this more in the next chapter, tie the pieces of my argument together, and explain where I even conceived of this idea.

ADHD is not all bad. It is a superpower. We can adapt at lightning speed in a crisis. Fawning has allowed us the ability to assess a situation and address it quickly before it becomes a problem. I have had jobs that loved me and jobs that have hated me (well, managers). If there was a crisis, I would perform. The problem was not when I was doing something. It was when I had nothing to do. The phrase "if you've got time to lean, you've got time to clean" was the bane of my existence. Give me a list, I will complete it. Tell me to figure it out, and I might shut down or make more work.

A good example comes in the way the Baby Boomer generation tended to parent the Millennial generation. Parents would often tell the kids to do the dishes or go clean your room without teaching those skills or expectations. So, a Millennial would try and often make more work. An example would be in cleaning the room, the Baby Boomer was requesting the Millennial to tidy up things around the room to make it *look* cleaner. The ADHD Millennial would begin by tearing apart the closet to completely reorganize it. The Baby Boomer parents would come in some time later and be upset due to the ADHD child having created more of a mess when all they said was to clean the room.

This is a good example of bottom-up versus top-down thinking. Top-down thinking is "Here is how to solve this math question." Bottom-up thinking is "Why and how?" The child with ADHD needs more explanation to understand the process, but they also need it to motivate themselves for the purpose of the request. "I want it done" is not a good purpose to the child with ADHD. This often led to the belief that people with ADHD, even if not diagnosed, were lazy.

Laziness is a fundamentally flawed idea. People with ADHD are *not* lazy. They are *unmotivated*. If you want something done and you don't want to do it, then it is your responsibility to motivate the person you want to do it. This often did not happen. The cudgel of laziness as a moral failing was a primary motivator for some parents. This unfortunately worked against them, as people with ADHD collapse under the weight of shame and develop learned helplessness. ADHD responds better to positive feedback and validation rather than punishment.

Chapter 12
The NAC to ADHD through CPTSD

This chapter is the culmination of the information provided so far. Think of it as my mission accomplished on an aircraft carrier at the start of a war; if you know you know. It is clear that narcissistic abuse can cause PTSD in children, and this has been supported in research [36]. We can understand that abuse of any kind causes PTSD. Furthermore, PTSD, by its nature, is not genetic, and we often attribute it to other disorders despite the harms of PTSD sometimes being encoded in genetics (discussed in more in a later chapter). However, we shouldn't assume that due to this genetic factor abuse doesn't play a role, at least at some point in the line of disordered succession (heritability and epigenetic changes, also discussed more later).

This link of PTSD and abuse has also been found in the link with CPTSD. CPTSD is a long-term form of PTSD that forms over time in a relationship. In this chapter, I will attempt to draw connections between the pipeline of the NAC to the development of PTSD and CPTSD, where science has already shown a causal relationship. I will further explain my hypothesis that this pipeline leads to the development of ADHD, though this causal relationship cannot be proven based on current scientific data. For now, the connection between ADHD and abuse is only correlative. Though there are studies connecting ADHD to abuse, I look to further correlate it with the NAC.

Heir of Narcissism

What is ADHD, and why might it form through abuse specifically from narcissism or highly critical authority figures? In my treatment of clients with ADHD and in my own life, I have noticed a trend of people with ADHD having at the very least a highly critical parent or close family member with regular contact, if not a narcissistic caretaker. The symptoms of ADHD seem to resemble all avoidant symptoms of PTSD mentioned in previous chapters. Individuals seem to be seeking to avoid something through removing stimulation or increasing it to a degree where there is no space in their head for anything else.

I believe this gives us the first clue as to where to look for the cause of the avoidance in ADHD, which I believe to be a primary symptom of ADHD. Inattention is avoidance of what the mind wants to focus on (escape), and hyperactivity is the avoidance of the current state by flooding. These symptoms are also related to overstimulation that affects concentration and focus. The mind and body are a place to be avoided. We avoid things that are uncomfortable and uncontrollable. We avoid what is unsafe. In ADHD, the mind is unsafe.

What could make the mind of a person unsafe, and why does it not simply fade or heal in the therapeutic process? Imagine if somehow the voice of a highly critical person were to enter your own mind and repeat itself in your own voice. Every day, your mind is unsafe due to someone hurting you emotionally. This would make the mind unsafe. Some people are aware of this voice, and some only become aware through therapy or later when they catch it speaking. The reason it is not eliminated completely in the therapeutic process has to do with the fact that not everyone is even aware anymore of its existence. Some people hear it, some do not, and some learn to hear it later.

I have had clients state that the other day they heard the voice say some really mean things to them in their own internal monologue. This is not a hallucinatory voice; it is the voice of the individual in the cases I am referring to. This was also described in an episode of *The Place We Find Ourselves* podcast [37] when Gary was a guest, I believe the second time. He discusses hearing this voice for the first time in a long time. He noted hearing the words "you f*ing idiot" in his head and noting those were the words of a parent when he was younger, and not his own.

No child is born into this world with hatred in their heart, at least for themselves. We are taught to hate ourselves if we learn to do so. This often happens in the younger years before our "self" is more solidified. Young children are easy to do long-term harm toward. The strength of the self does not come until later and is heavily affected by those we trust, such as parents. I want to make sure to be clear that much of what I am describing is intentional harm to a child's ego or self rather than the unintentional times we might wound someone we care about. This is not from "good enough" parenting or even the "not great" parenting, but rather the projected self-hatred of the parent onto the child.

Children don't have the defenses of adults to ignore bad and inaccurate feedback. They depend on parents to show them what is true and what is not true. The NAC confuses this perspective for the child. Resilience develops more easily when a comforting figure is available to help teach self-soothing and provide an emotional anchor. The wounds I am talking about are the ones that don't often come with repair from this emotional anchor [38]. Emotional outbursts with new rules based on the unknown internal state of the narcissistic or highly critical parent causes confusion in a child who creates rules to try and follow despite having many contradict each other.

This is how this voice slips into the mind of the child. The defenses are only partially formed, and the resilience abilities are not being fostered. Emotional repair is not happening. A repetitive chorus of the abusive parent's voice echoes around the child's head until it becomes part of their own speech pattern, and they start saying these phrases to themselves. That can often be the key in identifying them, as repeated phrases that might not always fit the context can be trauma re-enactments. The voice repeats so many times it becomes automatic.

The automation of this voice or the discomfort in hearing what it has to say can also lead the child to flee from the voice in their own head through distraction and hyperactive movements. Sitting still in the quiet becomes burdensome. Boredom is an illusory secondary emotion that hides the mind's scream, "Escape!" The avoidance begins in the attempt to flee from our own minds. As our walls go up in protection over the years and our personalities solidify, we don't notice the infiltrator in our minds that seems to now be trapped. The NAC is so pervasive as an extension of the personality disorder that it can become a trapped part of the mind of a narcissist's or highly critical parent's child without anyone truly knowing it. And it is far less forgiving than a narcissist as it has no crowd to behave in front of.

This causes the behaviors of inattentiveness and hyperactivity to present at a much higher rate in direct correlation to the level of stress created from this abusive cycle and now the internalized abuse in the survivor's head. The maladaptive coping behaviors of inattention and hyperactivity are then shamed due to how they make the narcissistic or demanding person look as a parent. This shame only worsens the behavior and increases the buildup, instructing the person with ADHD to hold things in. Well, anyone can guess what happens when emotions are held in and a person attempts to control compulsive behaviors through suppression. They explode, explaining the resulting difficulty in future relationships that do not tolerate this type of behavior.

The person with ADHD often will try to be "good enough" to earn the approval of a highly critical parent or narcissist to avoid further harm. They can do this by learning the rules they are given during each outburst or shaming session. This is where the voice gets further ingrained into the head of the person with ADHD. They repeat repeatedly and try to live by those rules to an obsessive and compulsive level. The abuse becomes internalized, and the reaction is an attempt to control and escape. Sometimes when control and escape is not possible, the person with ADHD may lean into chaos as a distraction. Avoidant trauma survivors often feel more comfortable in chaos, as described by Tara Conner in her TEDx Talk where she told a story about the first time she used substances at a party. She describes using drugs in a bathroom with two people hooking up, a person throwing up, and another person cutting themself. Tara described this chaotic room as matching the chaos in her head for the first time in her life [39].

The treatments currently available for ADHD are often psychopharmacology through the prescription of amphetamines, norepinephrine reuptake inhibitors, and dopamine reuptake inhibitors. They help ADHD have more access to chemicals in the brain that are also available during comfort without the longer-lasting effects of healthy comfort. The basis of self-medicating and psychiatric medication is to comfort the person with ADHD through chemicals in their own brain. The behaviors of avoidance are an attempt to avoid pain and seek comfort. Yet, we continue to treat the symptoms rather than the source. Later I will discuss substance use in the context of ADHD and what each substance attempts to treat.

ADHD needs to be better studied in relation to the NAC. I say this through anecdotal evidence, which admittedly is not strong and could be said to be biased by my own experiences in life, which are similar. However, it was through the treatment of over 10 people within a year that I noticed and identified a lot of this information. So, I don't believe it should be cast away so easily. Some studies have found conflicting information, and therefore, more studies are needed, as shown in the limitations and discussion section of Stern et al. (2018) which *also* calls for more research [40].

Though the science is limited for this and similar approaches, it does exist. A 2016 study by Capusen et al. correlates childhood maltreatment with increased ADHD symptoms in adults [41]. I often refer to untreated ADHD as narcissism lite or an air of narcissism, as it has similar symptoms with different intentions when discussed further. A narcissist helps people to look good, and looking good makes them feel good about themselves for a time. Someone with ADHD might help people with higher self-esteem or self-worth so that worth can be reflected in the negative self-view of the person with ADHD. More specifically, a narcissist does something nice to get something, whereas someone with ADHD does something nice because it feels good, even if *only* done selfishly to feel good.

Often the narcissist will hold these goodwill gestures against the recipient. While that seems to occur sometimes with ADHD, it is not until they have an emergent emotional need that has been suppressed. Hailey Shafir on *Choosing Therapy* notes how these conditions and more can be confused due to overlapping symptoms, particularly with Narcissistic Personality Disorder (NPD) [42]. For example, both ADHD and NPD have issues in impulsivity, may bore easily and so look for thrills and sensations, have higher rates of drug and alcohol use than the general population, and may be more irresponsible, distractable, have poor time management, and have difficulty following through.

However, there are also some key differences. ADHD tends to have more dysfunction in cognitive processing, organization, and impairment in work and school, whereas NPD often struggles with social/emotional areas of life. NPD tends to have poor empathy, leading to more exploitation and abuse, seeks attention more, and tends to be more grandiose and arrogant [42].

Again, while they may look similar, the major difference behind the behaviors lies in intent. Narcissism often has a more malignant or malicious intent as payment for their generosity, whereas ADHD seeks to do good things to feel good about themselves while helping others. Narcissism goes beyond the good deed into what is owed, and ADHD oftentimes terminates debt following the supportive behavior, except in cases of poor boundaries. Duarte et al. (2024) notes that other studies have found as much as 29.8% comorbidity between ADHD and NPD, whereas they were only able to find 9.5% comorbidity [43]. This difficulty in identifying overlap shows how difficult it is to study ADHD and the nuanced differences between disorders that appear similar.

Part IV: Maladaptive Coping

Chapter 13
Substance Use and ADHD

Disclaimer: Substance use and abuse are not a healthy way of managing uncomfortable or painful emotions in life. They are referred to as maladaptive coping skills when they are used to cope in a way that is harmful to yourself and others. Substances are *not* good coping skills, and though I discuss them as coping skills, it is *not* an endorsement. If you or someone you know is struggling with substance use, please use the resources below.

SAMHSA's National Helpline is a free, confidential, 24/7, 365-day-a-year treatment referral and information service (in English and Spanish) for individuals and families facing mental and/or substance use disorders: 1-800-662-HELP (4357)

Or 988 Suicide & Crisis Lifeline (just dial 988 if in the US)

Before moving into the discussion of substance use specifics and the needs that are met, I want to note these are not the only reasons people engage in substance use. I'm identifying how these substances meet the needs of individuals with ADHD. There are many traumas out there that are comorbid with the traumas of emotional abuse. Sexual abuse is often found in substance use. This pain needs to be respected.

Heir of Narcissism

In a speaking engagement, Dr. Gabor Maté discusses the origin of the word "addict" [44]. An audience member asks about changing the word we use to refer to addicts. In response, he discusses the origin of the word "addict" as coming from addictus. Addictus comes from Latin and means a debt slave. He describes how this perfectly encapsulates addiction. I have met people who didn't know about neglect or emotional abuse. A person craves comfort and relief, willing to give anything. They do this so often that by the end they are only able to achieve momentary relief trying to be normal rather than seek comfort or even a high anymore. They have become indebted to the drug. Recovery often asks for rebuilding from the foundation and is thus not a simple ask of, "Can't you just stop?"

Addiction is not a moral failing. It is a societal one.

Addicts are traumatized children grown up. They are the members of our society that were failed by society. The reason we struggle to look at them in active addiction is they remind us of how we looked away many times before. I've never met an addict who has not had trauma. I remember a professor arguing that not all addicts had trauma and some just get traumatized after becoming addicts. That was a callous statement to make and gave that professor the excuse to look away. In ten years of working with people in recovery, I haven't met one without trauma.

Substance use and ADHD can be separated. They can also be diagnosed together, called one of two things depending on the treatment setting: Co-occurring disorders or Dual Diagnosis. In the mental health field, we use the term Co-occurring disorders. Dual diagnosis is often a term used in the addiction treatment world. There doesn't seem to be a difference in the two terms, other than what it might say about the team treating the person and which disorder is primary for treatment. Dual diagnosis leans toward treating addiction as primary and mental health as secondary. The term Co-occurring disorder in mental health settings often looks at the cumulative effect of the disorders and how they interact with each other.

Sometimes people who seek treatment in drug and alcohol programs will be labeled as "high psych" if their mental health symptoms are too problematic for the system to handle. They are often shifted back and forth from psych hospital to rehab over and over. The psychological effects of mental health disorders tend to be ignored due to limited training on how to treat mental health, even more limited than on how to treat substance use. This is just to give a picture of the system in which people with substance use disorders are treated and why it feels ADHD, Bipolar disorder, and Schizophrenia are often untreated in these settings and removed when they become problematic.

The limitations on treatment are not only limited to treatment for disorders like ADHD. The sciences have also struggled to study the causal relationship of the symptoms, where they come from, the root cause, and how to treat them. Zulauf et al. (2014) names many of the reasons for substance use in connection with ADHD, but it is unable to definitively determine a causal relationship for the use. It describes using to attenuate mood, gain sleep, improve attention and executive functioning, and manage emotions related to demoralization and failure [45]. These are all fairly good reasons why a person might use substances if they had ADHD.

Zulauf et al. also concludes that children with ADHD are at an increased risk of developing substance use disorders, and continuous medication management can help mitigate this risk, despite medication being a controlled substance [45]. Nicotine is also studied, likely due to its stimulant effect and the seeking of a stimulant by people with ADHD. I will address government and barriers to proper treatment of ADHD due to this fear of addiction in later chapters. Here, I will focus on the substances that are often co-occurring with ADHD symptoms.

Substance use disorders and ADHD run hand in hand, but not for the reasons most people might think. Many hear that a stimulant with a similar chemical structure and name to meth is used to treat people, including children, and assume that they are the same or these people are just getting high. People also assume that medication management of this disorder with these controlled substances will cause addiction later down the line. Studies have suggested that prescribed stimulants neither increase nor decrease the likelihood of substance use later in life [46]. These stimulants also do not work chemically in many people with ADHD the way they work in the average person.

I have even had cases where families feared the misuse of amphetamine medications due to having experience with individuals who would abuse the medication to initiate a manic episode in bipolar disorders. Stimulants certainly induce manic episodes for bipolar disorders. However, they make people with ADHD feel normal and quiet the noise in their head. The effect is completely different between the two. It would be like knowing someone who is allergic to strawberries and fearing a reaction from everyone else you met if they ate a strawberry. It's not the same. And in fact, it is harmful to treat ADHD improperly due to a personal fear. Think of the person with ADHD in this scenario as someone who is deficient in the vitamin strawberries provide.

Earlier, I referenced a speaking engagement from Dr. Gabor Maté where he discusses brain development and addiction. That video has a lot to do with addiction and the parts of the brain that are damaged through trauma in childhood development that lead a person into the world of an addiction [33]. These substances meet extremely specific needs in the brain.

I have spent my career trying to understand the link between childhood trauma and drug of choice. I worked as a therapist in both a co-occurring intensive outpatient program for three and a half years, followed by three years in an inpatient rehab, both overlapping with six years in private practice working with addicts, among other needs. My experience is not scientific evidence, but I have noticed trends over the course of treating well over 1,000 patients through those years in well over 3,500 group sessions, in addition to individual therapy sessions. This is just to say that my ADHD sought to understand thoroughly what needs these drugs met for my clients in the same way people with personality disorders are seeking for needs to be met. I can't say that I was more accurate than a person pretending to be psychic and using cold reading or if my information was correlated to the actual issue, but I understand the need.

In my experience and going through the ICD 10 list of disorders [47], I have seen some interesting trends. F10 Alcohol use disorders were often people who had negative self-esteem, a highly critical parent, and identified alcohol as a social lubricant. F11 Opioid use disorders seemed to have difficulty connecting and feeling connected with others. Some of these clients would report physical or emotional neglect in childhood. Sometimes this was due to being a high needs child whose needs were not or could not be met. F12 Cannabis use disorders made up less than 1% of all the cases I have treated. Cannabis can create a false sense of connection but often seemed used to inhibit long term memory, living in 30-minute increments and being able to forget or inhibit thought long enough to fall asleep or make life less painful if existence was pain for said client. These three substances deal heavily with connection.

F13 Sedatives, Hypnotics, Anxiolytics use disorders include benzodiazepines, barbiturates, and sleep medications. Benzos had the nickname of alcohol in a pill, while sleep medications were often abused for sleep in those who had PTSD intrusive symptoms that they wanted to avoid to get sleep, to the point of inhibiting the ability to dream. Few people I treated abused barbiturates. F14 Cocaine, F15 Other Stimulants, F17

Nicotine use disorders are all stimulants and often related to ADHD or PTSD self-medicating. More specifically, F13 fed a desire to escape for neurotypicals while stimulant use fed escapism for neurodivergent individuals, specifically with ADHD. Some of these drugs were used in combination for other effects I will address later.

F16 Hallucinogen use disorders, like F13, covers drugs used for different purposes. In all my time treating people, I have never met anyone addicted to LSD (acid), Psilocybin (magic mushrooms), or Mescaline (peyote). Ketamine, PCP, and Ecstasy were the drugs people tended to abuse in this category. Ketamine shuts the brain off, as seen in a study on sheep [48]. PCP is dissociative and can disconnect people from reality, leading to extremes in behavior. Ecstasy is another form of escape and used as a party drug. Though new research is showing the benefits of most of these hallucinogens in the process of treating trauma and treatment-resistant depressions, that research is beyond my scope and the scope of this book.

F18 Inhalants use disorders then covers anything that can be inhaled to get high, from glue to spray paint and other creative versions. I have treated very few of these individuals in my career, but when I have, they were people with severe trauma experiences, and these inhalants were described to numb and escape the pain for a while. Ease of access was also a factor in this specific use disorder. These users also often reported using many other substances, or in their words, "anything I could get my hands on." I have had clients in this category call themselves "dumpsters."

The combination effect I mentioned earlier refers to the use of alcohol and cocaine in combination, and in extreme cases opioids and amphetamines, to achieve the same goal. These patterns of substance use were utilized to self-regulate emotions, particularly in people who had chaotic childhood homes with either parental substance use, mental health issues, domestic violence, or insecurity in food/safety, often due to poverty. Substances were used to bring the person down with alcohol and opioids, then they would use stimulants to come up again. These clients would describe wanting to drink endlessly and using cocaine when they were too drunk, so they could continue to drink. It was a maladaptive form of emotion regulation.

I will specifically focus the next few chapters of this section on the use of Alcohol by itself, Cannabis, and Stimulants as to how they affect people and are used to meet the needs of ADHD specifically. As stated before, I have confirmed these mechanisms interacting through qualitative motivational interviewing, along with a psychodynamic style. This process was not scientifically able to determine a cause, but it was able to note high enough correlations that further study would be beneficial.

My ADHD mind is trying to understand patterns that have not been extensively discussed in research, or I am bordering on conspiracy theory. My brain wants to understand wholly specific concepts that draw its attention. I see a pattern of behavior mixed with rudimentary neurobiological understanding. This has all come together enough to make sense for me, searching from the basis of what need is to be met to the understanding of how the brain achieves the meeting of these needs and the triggers for those neurochemicals. Taking the basic idea of safety and seeing the paths in which many people find similar solutions to similar problems without knowing each other, the human brain is the primary common factor. This is only followed by human experiences.

A final word on addiction before moving on: It's not pretty. Manipulative behavior, lies, cheating, stealing, pain, heartbreak, etc. are all part of the disease. We might not have healed the pain before the children became adults, and it can be hard to watch addicts do what they do to get what their minds crave. If you can't hold empathy for an addict due to what they have done to you, don't. Let the professionals heal your loved ones with empathy and boundaries. Just don't add anything that would undo that work. Shame and guilt heal no one. I will discuss later how our government and treatment systems have failed them. It wasn't all on any one of us, but *was* on all of us.

Chapter 14
Alcohol

People with ADHD have a higher risk of substance use disorders, specifically a 43% risk of alcohol use disorders in the ADHD population [49]. Alcohol use disorder populations also have a higher-than-average rate of individuals with ADHD at 20% of the population of users. This is significant, as only about 6% of the population has alcoholism [50], and 4.4% of adults have ADHD [51]. Many articles on these subjects point to the genetic aspect of alcohol use disorders as a reason for this development, or the issues of a parent's use, or the impulsive nature of ADHD leading to excessive use. These don't explain the core question or the connections between these factors in understanding how they are related. Yes, we believe there is a genetic component in both alcohol use disorders and ADHD. Later I will discuss the link of epigenetics and how this might provide a more complete explanation, since genetics alone does not explain why some and not others, even in the same family, may be susceptible.

The core question I have been asking through this book applies here as well: What need does the substance meet, specifically for a person with ADHD? Alcohol is a depressant. That doesn't mean that it makes you depressed. It depresses or lessens the effect of other things. It can even depress depression. You might have seen this in a person who drinks too much and can't stop crying. Alcohol lowers depression's numbness, and the individual has access to the underlying emotions of sadness.

Alcohol slows things down and inhibits those top layer emotions and thoughts. A person who is happier drunk might have pain being suppressed. An angry drunk might have their inhibitions to express said anger suppressed. Alcohol inhibits the brain's ability to function properly. It would also inhibit a brain with maladaptive thinking patterns from functioning in the maladaptive way, depending on what is affected. However, this inhibition is not always positive and comes at great cost to the body when used in excess or used to achieve these goals at all. This becomes self-medicating, self-soothing, or emotion regulation using a substance rather than the development of the emotional skills needed.

So, what needs does Alcohol meet in a person with ADHD? Remember earlier when I discussed how the voice of the narcissistic or highly critical abuser can get into the head of a person and my belief that this is what can lead to ADHD? Alcohol shuts that voice up, or at least makes it less audible in the head of a drunk individual. Alcohol slows the mind down and stops the negative self-talk for some people who drink. This is not to say that drinking enough and alone would not cause that voice to come back, but primarily the voice quiets when inebriated. The explanation of a social lubricant is congruent with this idea.

Many alcoholics I have treated over the years discuss how alcohol is used so they can be more comfortable in social situations. However, the story always ends up the same way: with the alcoholic drinking alone with no intention of social interaction. How does this make sense? A person claims to drink for social interaction and then ends up not wanting to be around others and still needing to drink. I think the common factor is the negative self-talk of the narcissist or highly critical person in their heads making it more difficult to socialize. The alcohol inhibits this voice and allows them to socialize, but the goal was never *really* to socialize. The goal was to get out of their own head or to make their own head safe. Alcohol does this without the need to socialize, and thus alcoholics end up drinking alone, as the need is met.

Alcohol is often also used to tolerate intolerable situations for people who abuse it. Some individuals with alcohol use disorder maintain relationships with highly critical or narcissistic parents even into adulthood. I have seen multiple cases through the years of adult children expected to visit and spend time with highly critical parents only to be berated over and over again about their shortcomings. I have seen people regress in treatment following every visit with these parents. Alcohol becomes a remarkably effective and yet maladaptive coping skill to maintain a relationship filled with shame and guilt without having to face the fear of abandonment or shame of going no contact with a parent.

The hyperactive mind is the mind in which the negative voice of the critical parent lives in our own words. Alcohol slows down the mind and can lead to the numbing or silencing of this voice. However, alcohol also limits inhibitions in the frontal lobe. These inhibitions could be said to help prevent believing what the negative self-talk is saying. In individuals with ADHD, alcohol can worsen the symptoms of hyperactivity despite being a depressant [52]. A person who is drunk cannot become not drunk through anything other than time, and time is a luxury a person without inhibitions does not often have.

People with ADHD are also more likely to abuse substances while having a poorer sense of interoception. That is, people with ADHD are less sensitive and less aware of internal stimuli, meaning it can take more deliberate stimulation for a person with ADHD, similar to many other types of neurodivergent individuals, to feel something or notice something. This means one or two drinks might not even be felt by a person with ADHD. They might not notice any internal changes with the introduction of normal amounts of alcohol and will need to drink to excess to achieve the desired sensation.

This can be seen in many other behaviors of neurodivergent individuals. We will often engage in stimming to self-regulate [53]. Stimming can be anything from copying a noise in the environment to tapping, touching, or picking at the environment around us. The attempt to self-regulate leading to excessive use of maladaptive coping skills and risky behaviors to stimulate can also lead to issues of life expectancy. Life expectancy in people with ADHD is almost 13 years less than the average [54]. This brings the average age of around 77-78 years down to about 64 years. The increase in risky behaviors and maladaptive coping skills are strong signs for this reduction.

There is also the belief in the drug and alcohol addiction treatment world that abstinence is the key to sobriety. In people who are capable of avoiding substance use, avoiding the effect on inhibitions, this might be true and even lead to better results. However, sobriety may also cause an issue for individuals with ADHD. The treatment medication for ADHD is a drug that is often abused by other addicts. Rehab doctors are less trusting in someone asking to be medicated with a controlled substance due to the nature of addiction. In a rehab with at least 115 beds and treating alcohol use disorder, with at least 20-25% of those individuals having ADHD, you would expect to see at least a handful of people being prescribed the proper medication. However, in my experience, only one or two people in the rehab at a time were prescribed Adderall.

This would mean that the treatment methods often work against best practices of treatment due to undiagnosed individuals and those who are believed to abuse the substances. Life can be hard for people with ADHD, especially in the seeking of treatment for substance use disorders due to these conflicting beliefs that lead to them being improperly treated clinically. They are treated as if they are lying, and each individual person in their treatment team might have different opinions about the treatment regimen, so that even if they are being treated properly, they can receive shame.

The danger in this treatment model is that it ends up reinforcing the critical parent. Rehabs treat a lot of people at a time with small staff numbers per shift. People acting out due to their psychological needs are not often tolerated very well and tend to be shamed into behaving through sheer emotional will, despite understanding addiction is not a moral failing or failure of willpower. Therapists can be bogged down by paperwork, leaving others to manage these behaviors. I once had a CEO who said the real therapy starts after 5 pm when the therapists would leave for the day. He was a big proponent of people in recovery helping each other, but this was also the attitude that led to ignoring mental health symptoms despite being a dual-diagnosis facility.

Substance use treatment leaves a lot to be desired in the United States. It is often referred to as drug and alcohol treatment, as if alcohol is not also a drug and killing in a gruesome way. Alcohol is one of the only detoxes that can kill a person. The primary treatment is for substance use, with mental health often treated only when it interferes with treatment of the addiction, rather than as a reason for the addiction. ADHD is very disruptive to the group therapy process that takes up most of the treatment day unless a facility is truly prepared to support people in all their issues. A co-occurring program that addresses both mental health and addiction is important for the treatment of those in these groups.

Chapter 15
Cannabis

The same question should be asked here that is asked in the previous chapter: What need does cannabis meet in people with ADHD? The answer in its most simplistic form would be to reduce hyperactivity and soothe the perception of the person with ADHD. By this I mean that cannabis is known to calm those who use it. It can slow down the thought process and help with sleep issues, specifically by the people who use it and claim it as a need for these reasons. It also has a specific effect on memory; short term memory struggles to convert into long term memory while high on cannabis.

When I am discussing memory in this chapter, I am specifically referring to recall of explicit memory. There are three classifications of recall memory that I will refer to by name when discussing them: long-term, short-term, and working memory. Long-term memory is what we think of when we think of recall memory. It is the movies, pictures, or thoughts of past events that we can recall when we want to remember something. However, this is the last stage of explicit memory. The other stages are working memory, which tends to last about 30 seconds, and short-term memory, which lasts about 30 minutes. Anything that is not converted into the next stage by the end of 30 seconds is dumped like RAM in a computer. Short-term memory acts like working memory, except in 30-minute intervals.

Heir of Narcissism

I will focus much of my attention on short-term memory to explain the need cannabis meets in people with ADHD. People with ADHD live in their own heads with omnipresent racing thoughts and negative self-talk, if they are aware of it. As discussed earlier, some people with ADHD follow urges to avoid without even being aware of the discomfort. Time stuck in a head with a voice that is critical and abusive is painful. Time then becomes painful. How can a person with ADHD make time less painful? Live in 30-minute intervals with no memory of the previous pain. This is basically why we use certain kinds of anesthetics to prevent the memory of the pain or to allow people to dissociate through it.

Thirty minutes of pain is also not particularly bad compared to a lifetime of it. And if you don't have to remember the pain that you have experienced, you might be able to accept it more. Cannabis allows this to happen in a person with ADHD. They don't have to experience the passage of time, as they forget what it felt like in the previous intervals and get to start almost fresh each new interval. The ADHD mind does not have to focus on or escape any form of thought, as it will be gone soon. They get to be free of care, worry, shame, and guilt for a time. This is a primary need that cannabis meets for people with ADHD.

One study found a link between the severity of ADHD symptoms and the usage of cannabis, implying an underlying connection of self-medicating behavior [55]. It's not clear in the research whether cannabis is beneficial in the long term for the treatment of ADHD. Based on my understanding of the symptoms and the effects of cannabis, I would venture to guess that it would be effective at treating the symptoms of the moment while doing nothing in developing long-term coping skills or support systems, similar to catharsis.

In an article for the Children and Adults with Attention Deficit/Hyperactivity Disorder (CHADD)'s *Attention Magazine*,

David Teplin discusses the acute use of cannabis and the effects on increasing dopamine in the short term while long-term effects blunt said dopamine [56]. This reinforces the aspects of any form of maladaptive self-medicating practice in that it is temporary in relief while limiting the system of relief from long-term benefit. Using a substance to manage any emotional issue is almost always going to lead to some form of chemical dependence. Cannabis is no different despite the lack of any withdrawal symptoms present in substances like alcohol or opioids.

As discussed earlier, ADHD is a processing disorder and an emotion regulation disorder to the distresses of maladaptive processing. Simply denying any effectiveness to these substances is taking away a coping skill without offering an alternative. This leads to the difficulty in treating a cannabis user who might be using through the process of treatment. Treatment tends to be inhibited or even nullified by mind-altering substances including alcohol. Distress tolerance discussed in Dialectical Behavioral Therapy (DBT) would be a much more effective form of coping, but a person has to be able to be sober to experience the process working in conventional treatment, not discounting recent research on hallucinogens in treatment.

A secondary use for cannabis for individuals with trauma and/or ADHD would be to treat sleep issues and anxiety issues that might prevent sleep. People with ADHD often have trouble falling asleep due to racing thoughts, avoidance of dreams/nightmares, and sudden energy to focus late at night. The racing thoughts and sudden focus are similar symptoms and likely because no one else is awake and it might be safer, or the person with ADHD is alone in their head and wants to focus on anything other than recounting the day. Cannabis use can help reduce these issues.

Cannabis can also be used to manage anxiety, especially if medication worsens it. Cannabis use to manage anxiety is not a perfect long-term solution, as it is a form of emotional dependence on a substance and a maladaptive, avoidant coping skill. Cannabis also needs tolerance breaks, or a pause in use to allow the body to return to a normal tolerance, if it is to be used relatively regularly so that the potency is still effective in treating the issues it is being used for. Tolerance breaks have no set period and may be from 48 hours to 21 days. An inability to engage in a tolerance break might be a sign of trouble.

This chapter is not my attempt to advocate for the use of cannabis, as it is the least effective treatment for ADHD in the long term through avoidance-based coping skills. I simply want to explore the reason a person would be drawn specifically to cannabis use in relation to an ADHD diagnosis and symptoms. It seems to me there may be a connection between this desire to avoid and escape that is associated with the use of cannabis in ADHD. The inherent memory deficit effects of the chemicals on the brain seem to be desirable along with the disruption in the internal self-talk dialogue due to the inconsistency in memory past short term and even in working memory at times.

No drug is safe, and cannabis is not legal in all 50 states, let alone federally at this time. Medical cannabis and recreational cannabis from states that regulate it might be a safer option, but even legality cannot protect a person from addiction (see alcohol). There have also been discussions about cannabis use and the development of psychosis in recent years. Psychosis is a disconnect from reality in the form of hallucinations and/or delusions. Hallucinations are any of the five senses sensing something not there for others. Delusions are beliefs that despite all evidence to the contrary a person still believes due to an emotional sense that it is true. Conspiracy theories often border, if not dive into, delusional territory. Hallucinations are often externalized experiences the brain projects into the world and processes as if they had activated the sensation. It is best to seek treatment for first episode psychosis and repeated episodes.

There is also the Hearing Voices Network that practices a more positive response to these symptoms.

I am not caught up on this science and won't speak to it now, but any usage of any substance can cause in specific people what is called substance-induced psychosis. If cannabis has induced a psychotic episode, it is likely no longer safe for that person to use anymore.

Cannabis used to always be called the gateway drug, but the only gateway cannabis created was being sold by the same person who also had opioids, crack, and meth. If the pain is great enough, people will do anything to ease it.

Chapter 16
Stimulants

Stimulants are often looked down on by society, and this stigma follows people with ADHD from the resistance to diagnosis knowing what will be prescribed through the everyday use of a substance that would make anyone else manic. This is unfair pressure, shame, and guilt added to people who are already suffering the negative effects of those feelings cast on them throughout their lifespan that led to the need for these substances. Stimulants range from caffeine in chocolate or coffee to nicotine in tobacco or vapes to cocaine/crack and through methamphetamines. They all tell the brain to release dopamine.

Dopamine is a chemical in the brain that is responsible for vitality, curiosity, and motivation. Dopamine is also one of what are called catecholamines which also include epinephrine and norepinephrine. The latter two are utilized in the fight or flight response, and specifically norepinephrine is a target of more current Selective Norepinephrine Reuptake Inhibitors (SNRI's) and Norepinephrine and Dopamine Reuptake Inhibitors (NDRI's) for depression and/or comorbid ADHD. People with ADHD do not completely lack dopamine or these other chemicals, but the brain does not readily release the chemicals, and the number of dopamine transporters in someone with ADHD is higher. These transporters take the dopamine out of the synapse between brain cells. These chemicals are important to life and for a creature's motivation for survival.

One study found this connection of motivation for survival. Scientists were able to engineer out a precursor enzyme of catecholamines, tyrosine hydroxylase, in mice [57]. This led to the mind being unable to create DOPA and thus not have access to the catecholamines [58]. The mice had no dopamine and no urgency to survive, and so starved to death over four weeks. Even placement next to a food bowl would not rouse these mice enough to eat for survival. They lacked motivation and urgency to eat despite other processes that might have been going on in their body [57].

Can people with ADHD get addicted to stimulants? The short answer is yes. In fact, people with ADHD might even seek out stimulants before they realize they are seeking them out. It is common for 12-step people in recovery to walk around with large cans of energy drinks and drink at least two of them a day. Stimulants cause the brain to release dopamine. This dopamine can help people with ADHD focus, quiet their minds, and reduce hyperactive behaviors. Watch any video online of a newly diagnosed adult with ADHD taking stimulant medication for the first time. They describe silence and peace and often cry. This can be a feeling to chase due to the mechanisms of stimulants and the development of the chemicals in the brain.

When a person takes a stimulant, there is a rush of dopamine released in the brain. This sensation in the average person or to a greater effect in a person with bipolar disorder will cause a sense of euphoria. However, these stimulants are not regulated and will often release more dopamine than the brain can replace in a given time. This leads to deficits of dopamine with an unchanged desire for more dopamine. This is why they say you will always be chasing the first high with any of the stronger stimulants. The rush of dopamine will never match this again, but your brain will chase it anyway, all while depleting the dopamine through a war of attrition.

People with ADHD work differently, as they may have a surplus of dopamine in the brain that is not being utilized by the proper mechanisms. Studies actually show that people with ADHD that are treated with stimulants have a lower risk of addiction to them than those who do not have ADHD [59]. Another study explored the misuse of ADHD medication on college campuses and noted that the misuse was likely in correlation with the severity of the symptoms [60]. This study suggests the accommodation system was inadequate, or absence in care for the disability of ADHD symptoms as a reason for abuse.

Again referencing Dr. Gabor Maté, ADHD is like the brain has a three-lane highway in all directions with a traffic cop in the middle. The stimulant helps to arouse the traffic cop to allow for the organized directing of traffic [33]. These stimulants help the mind of a person with ADHD regulate and organize their thoughts more like a line rather than a crowd all trying to fit through the same door. Often, my thoughts will move so quickly that I fear I might forget what I am saying before my mouth is able to verbalize the process aloud. Stimulants bring order and help quiet the mind, like the shift from a crowded theater full of people talking suddenly falling silent into the first draw of the orchestra's violin.

I worked in a gas station when a certain energy drink came to market at $1.99 per can, or $2.11 after tax. My friends were all drinking two of them to feel buzzed. I drank two and felt nothing. I drank two more and felt nothing other than slight for my $8.44. Coffee has never had a noticeable effect on me. Surge was my lifeblood in childhood, and I miss it every day I remember it existed. Something about pseudoephedrine, a common decongestant in my childhood, always made me feel better than any other medication. I didn't know what it was, but something about stimulants always seemed to make things clearer and calmer. I had no idea that I had ADHD at the time. I just knew I felt more normal and had access to the energy in my tank when I was on some kind of stimulant.

The need that is met by the stimulant and the reason it is the most common prescription for ADHD is the ability of the brain to focus and organize thoughts and emotions. A person with ADHD is often overwhelmed even when they don't realize it. We act out on pain we don't even remember we have sometimes. Perhaps stimulants also provide us access to a more ready supply of fight or flight response in which we can feel safe enough to focus in addition to having motivation changes, sometimes mistaken with energy. ADHD might be characterized as a fear of deficiency. There is a constant thought in my head that revolves around the conservation of energy. I *have* energy. Sometimes I lack motivation to be able to use said energy even if I want to.

Stimulants are the drug of choice for the person with ADHD who wants to have access to their motivation. If it is abused, this access route gets shut off due to the brain not being able to keep up the supply to the demand. However, if used properly with the support of emotion regulation coping skills, a person with ADHD might be able to maintain a balance and operate in a more neurotypical way.

Substance use disorders also bring up an interesting point: ADHD and substance use are likely genetic in nature, and that has meaning when it is said so often in our world. Though I believe there is a genetic component, that component is likely closer to whether a person would like broccoli than to the presentation of eye color. I also believe that ADHD and addiction would have the same ability to be changed, though a bit more difficult than liking broccoli. The next section will address similar issues in the lack of research toward the cause of these genetic presentations and the barriers toward efforts to understand an origin.

Part V: Genetic Debate

Chapter 17
Nature v. Nurture

Anyone who has had an introduction to psychology class at any level of school has likely run across the classic argument of nature versus nurture. Nature is genetics, and nurture is the environment and relationships around you. This argument was always a setup in any class that I had taken, as it always starts out innocently enough by asking the class whether it believes nature or nurture has more impact on the development and presentation of how a person turns out. The professor will lead the discussion for a while, calling on everyone and letting them speak, only to come in at the end and basically sound the proverbial buzzer notifying everyone that they are wrong.

"It is both," the professor will often say. This is actually the answer to most questions in psychology that offer a false dichotomy, unless you are in social psychology (then the answer is always cognitive dissonance). The answer is almost always both. It is our genetics and our interactions with the environment as we grow up. However, it often seems like nature gets blamed for anything we can't find a way to change or counter in people, such as ADHD, Schizophrenia, Bipolar, Personality disorders, addiction, and more. I will address this issue more in the next chapter. For now, we can focus on the basics of the argument.

Heir of Narcissism

The argument of nature versus nurture is often portrayed in a way that forces us to project aspects of ourselves and our own beliefs onto the idea. Neither nature nor nurture care about us or are determined to affect us any more than the other. We are not so significant that the universe has it out for us or that our genetic line wants to compete with said universe. In fact, they often work hand in hand in the presentation of our genetics based on the environment. Our minds are rather good at adapting to our world. Our genetic code in this context is not exactly changing based on evolution in this abbreviated time. Rather it is changing based on expression triggers in the environment, leading to what we call epigenetics, which we will come back to in Chapter 19.

Sometimes it is difficult to tell what aspects of ourselves are due to nature or nurture. One way to separate nature from nurture is through twin studies. Psychology Today discusses how scientists estimate the variation of a specific trait based on the differences in identical and fraternal twins [61]. Twin studies can be helpful in this way, but they have limitations. These studies are not perfectly generalizable to the greater population and can actually vary due to said populations. The bottom line is that it is exceedingly difficult to determine what can be nature and what can be nurture, since we have gained greater understanding of the influence of each on the other.

Development of a person is often based on the challenges faced in early life, whether genetic or environmental. It is struggle that forces us to adapt, and humans do this so well, I tend to say it is near perfect for the circumstances. People who have been traumatized have learned to live in trauma-rich environments. The disordered aspect of the trauma is often triggered by normal and relatively safe environments. The person can become uncomfortable and lack the struggle to force our adaptation skills in this activated state. It seems easier for a human to adapt to struggle than it is to adapt to peace.

ADHD in the way I have discussed throughout this book could be seen in a similar vein. It is perfect at managing crises while avoiding internal negative thinking through constant intellectual or physical movement. In my opinion, ADHD is developed as a reaction to surviving a house with a person who makes your own head unsafe and creates a cycle of chaos so pervasive that peace is never expected to last. In fact, peace becomes triggering as an omen of what is to come. The modern paradigm often attributes ADHD to genetics, but I see it far more as behavioral due to how well it is adapted to the environment of the individual.

What I would consider nature is the brain structure and how humans use it in the development of adaptations. We all start with a similar structure that changes through neuroplasticity caused by our experiences. The physical structure of our brain created through the reading of genetic code is then modified based on our patterns and experiences in the world daily and can occur in as little as two weeks.

Clients in the recovery world would often resist treatment, especially from someone who has never had an addiction, due to believing that that person could never understand how they think. To a degree that makes sense. However, we are all human and have the same basic needs: safety and survival. Humans adapt by avoiding pain and seeking comfort. That is the human condition. Harry Harlow sought to know if food or comfort was more important to primates, so he built two monkeys out of chicken wire and covered one in terry cloth (but had no food) while the other had food (bottles of milk) but no comfort. The young monkeys would move from the terry cloth mother to the wire mother only to feed, then spend the majority of their day in the comfort of the terry cloth mother [62].

I saw the aspects of nature and nurture truly show in the form of treating addiction. I can't tell you how many clients I have had in my office who have used the exact same phrases word for word and yet have never met one another and never ran in the same circles. "I know what I need to do, I just need to do it" was often said to me before a person signed out of the facility against medical advice. Similarly, "I am not like these other people. I can stay sober this time" was often said to me before an AWOL, labeled in a chapter as being terminally unique in the big book of Alcoholics Anonymous [63].

How and why would so many people say such similar things to me, most of the time word for word? Addiction also was not the only place this happened in treatment. I can pinpoint trauma the second a person overly beats themselves up for responsibility in their own trauma with similar phrases. I can hear an abuser's words through their survivor. We are not all so unique in physical structure despite having a unique experience of life. Our development is partially limited by our experiences, as can be seen in the phenomenon of "wild children" or "feral children."

There are many documented examples of wild or feral children throughout the history of humanity. These children were a phenomenon of ending up alone in the world and somehow surviving from an early age, despite nature and nurture, with little to no contact with the modern human world. They are what we might think of when someone says they were raised by wolves. However, not all stories involve supportive packs that would protect the child, and instead they survived some other way on their own. The two cases I will be discussing are Genie born in 1957 and Victor born around 1788. Victor is one of the most well-documented cases of this phenomenon, and Genie is an American-born person who developed these traits through severe neglect and isolation in a home.

Victor was found in the woods of France sometime between age nine and eleven. He was seen as a perfect example to be studied based on Jean-Jacques Rousseau's theories about nature versus nurture and the need to raise children outside the influence of society [64]. Victor was not what Rousseau imagined, as he did not interact the way people were expecting and only seemed to care about eating, sleeping, and privacy. A contemporary psychologist decided he was faking it and that he was an irredeemable idiot. Luckily Victor was not assigned to that psychologist for care and documentation.

Victor was assigned to Dr. Itard, who named him and worked to study and teach Victor. Dr. Itard tried enlisting others to teach Victor to speak, but over the course of five years, Victor was able to identify simple words but never learned to speak. Victor's senses were attuned differently than those around him. He was unaffected by snuff, reached into boiling water, and had no reaction to the firing of a gun. However, the cracking of a walnut sent him into a flight-like response [64]. These attuned senses seem targeted toward the danger he would have faced surviving in the wild rather than in society. In this case, the nature argument falls relatively flat for development, unable to explain these differences in response to dangerous stimuli. There also seems to be a critical window in which nurture can be effective.

Genie is the other child of neglect who had similar traits to the wild children found throughout history. She was kept in a room alone until she was 13. I will leave the story out due to the extreme nature of neglect and the triggering story in which she came to be found, but you can find it in my references. Genie was brought out of the home through child protection services, who worked with her in an attempt to rehabilitate her. Genie's ability to learn language seemed limited, and she struggled to form sophisticated sentences despite her teacher noting her sophistication in storytelling through artwork [65]. This story reinforces Noam Chomsky's criticism of behaviorism in 1959 when B.F. Skinner was unable to define how behaviorism explains the acquisition of language (behaviorism being the far side of nurture).

Heir of Narcissism

Nature versus nurture is the psychological version of the argument of determinism versus indeterminism or fate versus free will. I was very much a free will absolutist in my early years of life and into the early years of my career. That is until I spent time treating people in impoverished communities and saw the effect of intergenerational trauma on the ability of people to break free of the system. This idea is also discussed in the studies of how the zip code a person is born into can determine the limit to their opportunities in life [66]. That is not to say a person can't escape their circumstances or find their way out of poverty or less fortunate circumstances. However, if I asked you to find a therapist today, do you know how you might go about that process? Or maybe apply to college and receive financial aid that you would be able to pay off before you retire? Who taught you how to do that?

Search engines are indeed free, but you first need to know what to ask. There is a form of limited free will in which our free will is limited by the choices we know to make and the questions we know to ask. That might be nature or nurture, but being taught new questions is absolutely nurture. So, nurture would be the key to access free will. But again, free will is limited by what you know to ask, and thus is just a wider sandbox of determinism. This sandbox can of course be modified if you happen to know or can afford a carpenter with a supply of sand.

I believe the development of ADHD is due to many factors associated with genetics. It could be a person's tolerance to negativity or their resilience to trauma. Perhaps they have a robust system to develop the neural chemicals such as dopamine and ability to use them and some sort of natural resistances to maladaptive changes through neuroplasticity. However, it is difficult to identify these possibilities, as I have not seen many studies that confirm the attributing systems in the development of ADHD, outside of the ones I have described, which are linked more with environmental and behavioral factors.

Aspects greatly associated with the symptoms of ADHD relate to trauma and the fight or flight response systems in the body. They are modified by changes in the environment and are strongly changed through relationships with others. A secure support system and attachment doesn't seem as often to lead to ADHD; one such study found connections between insecure/disorganized attachment and ADHD in school-aged children (though the author does report a possible conflict of interest due to receiving royalties from a parenting book) [67]. It would appear that indeed attachment seems to line up with the presence of ADHD and include symptoms such as rejection sensitive dysphoria. Attachment style could be viewed as a strong influence on ADHD if not part of the development.

Chapter 18
Genetic Barrier

Genetic attribution in causal relationships is often a throwaway dead-end line in the process of explaining what causes something. It often feels as though a genetic cause means that it can't be changed and therefore requires no more thought. This is a frustrating pattern that happens in studying behavior and disorders in people. It's an easy dumping ground for what we can't explain or develop a hypothesis for. It could even be said to be a defense of psychological study, due to the high burden of being referred to as a "soft science" by anyone who has never studied the methods. Genetics is a blooming field in the world of science, and techniques like gene editing have even begun to be used clinically to correct things like blindness, deafness, and hemophilia. The seeming excuse of genetic origin as a reason to look no further is quickly disappearing as science forges ahead into the modification of human genetics.

I have offered glimpses at the idea of epigenetics throughout this book, and in the next chapter I will address it more fully. For this chapter, I will focus on the maladaptive use of genetics as a barrier to further study when it shouldn't be. Genetics absolutely can be a *part* of the explanation and play a reciprocating role with the environment, as we now understand through the nature versus nurture debate.

Heir of Narcissism

One of the issues that comes up in the study of genetics or performance of part of a person's brain is the ethics of modifying the person for research. Typically, to study these issues we need to find someone with an overactive version and someone with an underactive version of the element being studied. This is not always an easy task and thus can even make a genetic basis unethical to explore in humanity. And we can't always generalize the results of studies found in animals to people. However, in my opinion it should also be unethical to label the unexplained as genetic in order to avoid having to explain it. This behavior feels like discrimination against a disability that has no known cure and is being explained away as unworthy of the resources for study.

Which mental illness is genetic? That's a tough question, and it depends on how we define the terms. Are we asking if something that is genetic is automatic, has a chance of happening, or can be activated later by specific circumstances? There are genetic disorders that will cause an event if not stopped, such as types of congenital blindness. However, this doesn't seem to be the case for psychology as much as it seems a certainty in some physical conditions. Many of the issues with the disorders that are often described as genetic are due to the disturbance level of the person experiencing the symptoms. Therefore, we only see the forms where people struggle with the symptoms enough to seek treatment and have a bias in the sample set.

Eleanor Longden discovered her psychosis as a hallucinated voice that developed in her college years. She discussed not feeling disturbed by this voice until she told a friend who had her go to the school psychologist, which led her to the hospital system, and her mental health deteriorated from there [68]. It would be interesting to know whether her lack of disturbance by the voice would have ever even led to a diagnosis if she had never been told it was abnormal. Starting college can also be stressful. Was this genetic, environmental, or genetics activated by the environment? We don't necessarily know that unless we know if a gene is there, on, and is turned on or off by the environment. We are not there yet.

Even in the cases where genetics has a strong role in the development of whatever is being studied, it is important to consider the environment and what might add to the strength of these results. One study examined the top 10 replicated findings from behavioral health and found that four of them were largely related to environment, not genetics. The authors further state it is thus important to understand how the environment can change sensitive genetics [69]. The days of ignoring both environment and genetics for the excuse of "it is what it is" are over. Science has a large responsibility to step up in the development of theory in behavioral and genetic interpretations.

Genetics can often be scapegoated as a reason something is the way it is and is unchangeable or inherently bad. We need look no further than the misuse of genetics in white supremacy. Genetics is often used to say specific groups of people with genetic differences in phenotype have an inherent lack of some magical aspect of character or moral ability. I don't typically side with white supremacists and don't side with the idea that the color of a person's skin has anything to do with their behavior, other than the area in which they might have grown up due to institutional racism and the practice of redlining (creating areas in which racism stoked maladaptive survival behaviors to develop).

The big problem of psychology is the basis of our inability to determine the limits of mind and body. We don't even have the ability to understand what in the brain specifically makes up the personality or the self that ultimately makes the decisions for any one individual. It might be hubris to try and blame genetics for the complicated amalgamation of so many parts we can't even explain. The origin of the term psychology comes from the Latin study of the soul/mind. Previous generations of humanity might have understood this soul to reside in and be made up of the mind. We have since replaced the term soul with the word self in everyday usage, but that doesn't diminish the early understanding of the power of the area of our brain we call the mind and soul.

The brain is a complex thing in that it never quite works exactly how we believe it works. When we determine something in the brain works in a specific way, we can often find someone whose brain doesn't work in that way, possibly due to damage or difference in development. Lashley showed us this complex nature in action as he removed parts of mouse brains to view how it affected the ability to run a maze, which only slowed the process when removing tissue outside of the frontal lobe [70]. This study showed that the brain works in unexpected ways and has a higher order to thought outside of localized authority.

We know some areas of the brain are the centers for specific functions, but even through this lens many different areas carry multiple functions on different sides of said area. There are areas responsible for relaying sensory information, like the thalamus and the geniculate nucleus, among others. However, on the other side, there are areas such as the fusiform face area which we believe detects faces and Broca's and Wernicke's areas that are part of speech. Even when we think we know how one aspect of the brain works, we cannot generalize these understandings to the whole brain. The physical structure is developed based on a genetic recipe, but it is also influenced by how it is used through neuroplasticity.

Complex trauma is difficult to identify as a cause in behavior or presentation, as the barrier between genetic and environmental is further limited due to the encoding of trauma into our DNA. Evidence for this is building in ongoing research. For example, one study found the transgenerational transmission of DNA methylation changes from parents to children [71]; methylation is a heritable addition of a methyl group to part of DNA, which can alter how DNA is expressed [72]. This arises from environmental factors that affect our DNA that are then passed down and expressed through genetics in the next generation.

It would seem improper to utilize the idea of genetic changes or presentations of a person as unchangeable or less important to how we treat a disorder, as genes are influenceable through the process of epigenetics and the limitations of influence are not completely understood. Genes can change presentation based on the environment, as I will discuss in the next chapter, but they can also be changed through emerging gene therapy treatments. It would benefit the health treatment world to better understand the influence we can have on these changes through physical treatments and changes to the environment.

Chapter 19
Epigenetics and Changes in DNA

Epigenetics is the process by which gene expression is modified, and its study boils down to understanding how environmental factors can turn the expression of specific genes on or off ("epi-" is a Greek prefix meaning "on" or "over"). One way to think about epigenetics could be similar to the old stories of a person who has seen something so frightening their hair turns white. This could be due to changes in genetic expression caused by stress and the genetic makeup of the individual. The fear in the environment modified the expression of genes related to hair pigmentation, resulting in premature white hair replacing pigmented hair. Epigenetics is a newer idea in the world of science, and there is still much to be learned. We are still trying to understand it, and thus knowledge is limited (including this example on white hair).

On the surface, epigenetics may sound like genetic predisposition, but they're not quite the same. Genetic predisposition simply means that a person has the genetics that would cause a specific thing to happen and is more likely to have said circumstance happen in their lifetime. Epigenetics is similar, but the person won't necessarily develop the result of expression unless certain environmental factors are present. It is difficult to differentiate genetic predisposition and epigenetics from my level of understanding, and I don't want to misdirect anyone. I would encourage anyone to investigate the definitions themselves and try to understand.

Epigenetics could be an explanation for trait expression in large populations related to environmental factors. These changes often happen much faster than evolutionary changes and can apply to smaller swaths of the population as compared to the global population. One such change has been theorized by many who study trauma and addiction who have noted the development of substance use at a higher rate in populations of cultures that were targets of genocide. Addiction in general is likely a good explanation for epigenetics and can explain more why some individuals in families develop an addiction and others do not.

Biologically, each gene in a person's genome may either be expressed or suppressed, depending on a number of factors [73]. Expression relies on whether the blueprint (the gene) is available (accessible) to the process of the cell translating the gene into the product. When not being expressed, DNA can be tightly wound around proteins (called histones), making them inaccessible to this process, and thus they are not expressed. However, changes to the histones by attaching or removing various molecular groups (like methyl and ubiquitin groups) can alter how tightly DNA is wound, making it more or less accessible to that process, like winding or untangling Christmas lights. These groups may be added or removed by many factors, including changes in the environment or experiences of the person.

Epigenetics is a possible factor in the development of ADHD or substance use disorders based on a genetic component that is often discussed and an activating environmental event such as complex PTSD developed through the NAC. Many mental health conditions such as neurodivergence are identified as having a strong genetic origin. However, as I have discussed so far, it appears there are environmental factors that would promote the development of these symptoms. Triggering the fight or flight response can eventually lead to the development of trauma, if circumstances are right. The continued cycle of abuse in complex trauma can possibly lead to the development of ADHD-like symptoms based on which responses are activated and on environmental factors.

This is possibly seen in the presentation of the different specific criteria of ADHD diagnoses in individuals. The environment is a heavy influence on these presentations. One member of a family with a narcissistic or highly critical parent might develop ADHD and another member might not. This could be due to the differences in experiences of each family member. In the years between the birth of other children in the same family, each family member can have unique responses to what seem like similar experiences. These responses are often based on family position, responsibility, expectations, and unique interpretation of a given event. For example, when one member of the family aligns with a perpetrator, another may align with the victim, leading to a wildly different experience. The child with ADHD might also be more prone to develop alcoholism later in life due to the situation at home and depending on access to alcohol and a support system, which can also change over time. In my experience, this does not limit the other child from developing alcoholism but makes the person with ADHD more prone to it.

In psychology, we call these counters to unhealthy outcomes protective factors. Trauma is not traumatic to everyone involved. Risk factors can lead to negative outcomes and the development of traumatic response, possibly in relation to epigenetics. Protective factors include a healthy support system you can turn to, good coping skills in comfort and self-regulation, and future goals you might want to achieve and focus toward in challenging times. Risk factors include isolation, maladaptive coping skills, poor self-efficacy, an external locus of control and feelings of powerlessness, low autonomy, and anxious or fearful attachment to caregivers.

These are factors that would benefit or hinder a person's development of healthy or inhibitory genetic presentations in response to the environment. For example, it has been shown that mindfulness helps to lengthen telomeres. Telomeres are the tail-like, repetitive DNA sequences at the end of chromosomes and have been linked to life expectancy. Mindfulness for some reason helps to lengthen these structures and aid in the safe replication of our cells. Think of a zipper. A zipper that has strong stoppers on either end to keep the zipper from breaking is likely to last longer than a zipper with no stoppers. Our DNA replication is affected by mindfulness, and we are developing a better understanding of how to further influence our genetic presentations with epigenetics.

This understanding is the strongest answer to the nature versus nurture question that I think deep down we all somewhat understood to some degree. It is both and always has been both. People growing up in negative circumstances have a harder time than those growing up in positive circumstances. People who are the progeny of generations of negative circumstances have more physical issues over their lifespan. The Johns Hopkins Center for Indigenous Health discusses the impacts of intergenerational trauma on the physical health of indigenous populations in the US [74]. These factors compound over time and are passed down through our DNA to those who come after us. The research shows the effects of these harms to a culture over time.

One event in the winter of 1944/45 during World War II has been studied as an example of a historic trauma that led to negative effects in later generations. The Dutch famine affected the community, including pregnant women, due to the conditions of the world and the war limiting the transport of food. The studies that followed looked at the long-term effects on newborns and others in similar situations. Those born after the famine had higher rates of schizophrenia, stress sensitivity, and obesity [73]. It would seem the epigenetic change in the presentation of DNA handed down in these cases was almost preparing individuals for harsh conditions, and survival-based mechanisms were more readily activated.

This would also make sense that those born into situations in which survival is not guaranteed would be ready and able to adapt to conditions with a focus on survival rather than longevity. I say this due to the negative long-term effects that survival mode can have on a body stuck at that level of stress for an extended period of time. It would help a person survive for the short term versus dying quickly while also lessening the health of the person over a longer period. It is no wonder so many oppressive cultures refer to those they oppress as savages or primal when they have forced entire populations into this state of complex, chronic trauma; they activate a survival response and then call it savage.

The oppression of the highly critical parent on the person with ADHD seems to lead to these changes in which the mind is constantly working and little break is given. In fact for a person with ADHD, breaks are often more traumatic and anxiety-inducing, as at least one study has shown following the pandemic and quarantine of large swaths of the population [75]. People with ADHD had too much time in their heads alone for a long period of time and possibly ran out of things to do. Puzzles sold out, plant seed prices skyrocketed, sourdough starters were started and abandoned. These might have been screams for help from the tormented isolates. Imagine being in a silent room, attempting to hear any danger approaching. The feeling that danger is coming doesn't go away with silence and can be traumatizing. We will likely see the effects of epigenetics on future populations in relation to this pandemic and the ways in which they interact with each other.

Chapter 20
Protecting Ego

The proposed development of ADHD as a result of the NAC might be awkward for parents to hear, and there may be resistance to this idea, whether warranted or not. Many parents love their children unconditionally. Those are not the parents I refer to in the use of the NAC. The NAC is intricately connected to conditional forms of love and affection that are based on many things including the supply of validation to the parent. Highly critical people are not great at accepting criticism themselves, and so this chapter might be where they would burn or ban this book.

I don't treat children in my practice. That is by choice. I specialize in the realm of trauma and have unintentionally found myself in the substance use treatment world over the past ten years, as trauma often appears here too. That is not to say trauma is not present in children. In fact, that's the problem. Trauma is very much present in children who would come to see me specifically. The problem often was that these children had no power to speak up in their homes. When working with the children to have a voice, a highly critical parent could shut down months of work quickly and effectively silence their child with the threat of rejection.

I cannot treat children, because the powerlessness of their situation (that doesn't meet the standards for reporting abuse) is heartbreaking. I've spoken to parents about what I've seen, and they nodded their heads, seeming to understand, only to lash out in an equivalent way before the following session. Excuses of "well maybe if he wasn't lazy" or "she just doesn't try hard enough" or "I don't understand what's wrong with them, their sibling doesn't act like this" are all too common when helping children. A parent is the first and most important relationship in a person's life. They are the first engagement with the world, and we depend on them for food and comfort. We also hopefully learn these skills from them.

    A child's job is not to motivate themselves or comfort themself before it is taught to them. Parents are teachers, and children are dependent on those teachers being good at their jobs. No person is perfect, and I'm not trying to guilt any one person into believing they are terrible and there is no repair. I want to convey the message that when, as the person in power, we accept that those below us are suffering, then we can change that suffering into community and safety. Gen X parents that I have treated have shown the propensity to make this change, and I congratulate them, and even Baby Boomer parents who are able to do the same. Accepting responsibility for pain, even unintentional pain, can save years in therapy.

    It's not always easy to know where we go wrong in hurting others or even knowing that others were harmed by our behaviors. Trauma can cause us to act out in ways that are painful to the people around us while also giving us justification for acting out due to our pain. This cannot be an excuse. Invalidation does not make the pain disappear. In fact, it worsens the pain for the people we love. Codependency is a good example of this. Codependency is an intolerance of someone else's emotions being dissonant from your own and wanting to change that. This can often lead people who want to help to those helpers screaming at the person they wanted to help. We must be aware of our own pain to be able to see the impact on others.

Movies today created by Gen X and Millennials often have the theme of the parent apologizing. This is not a fluke. Most of these adult children want nothing more than for their parents to be able to be vulnerable and express they did the best they could, and it might not have been able to shield the child from the pain. I cannot express how healing a sit-down talk about ways in which a child might have been hurt can heal that child even as an adult. I posit this to many of my adult clients who fear their children will never forgive them: How would you feel if your parents were here right now and apologized for everything they did that hurt you through your life and let you know it wasn't about you or within your power to fix/stop/avoid?

Most people tell me they would forgive their parents on the spot and more easily forgive themselves for the guilt. There is this belief that if the oppressor were to take responsibility for their oppression that the oppressed would retaliate. The fear of "Cancel Culture" is the epitome of this idea. Most people who are canceled, own up to it, and genuinely apologize are uncanceled the same day. It is the "I'm sorry if" and other non-apologies that keep people canceled. Cancel culture is a sort of boundary to protect ourselves from those who do us harm, intentionally or not.

Cancel culture was a direct response to rape culture. In the age of healing, we believe the wounded. Sure, false reports do happen unfortunately, but it is far less common than you might think. Multiple studies have seemed to narrow false allegations to somewhere between 2-8%, and when criteria were corrected for "a clear and credible admission by the complainant" or "strong evidential grounds", these numbers were 2% out of 2,643 cases [76]. You may be confused why I am discussing sexual assault in the middle of a chapter about parenting. Assault is about power and control, oppression is the same, and traumatic parenting again the same.

I also discuss this due to a target of my idea in the origin of ADHD, the narcissist or highly critical parent. They are not great at accepting responsibility and will often claim false reports from the survivors of their trauma. If you pay close attention to the survivors of these reports, you might notice how self-deprecating the survivor is to themselves and how long they might have agonized over the idea of coming forward to report anything at all. One of the classic signs of a survivor of narcissistic abuse is self-blame and cognitively dissonant defense of the abuser. Follow this with the narcissist's projection and gaslighting, sprinkle in a little moving of the goal post, and you have the show we see so often on the news when a person is accused.

So, one of my main points in this section is that in the treatment of survivors of abuse, I am often combating the internalized voice of the narcissist or highly critical parent. I know its language and can hear it differently than I hear my clients. I wonder and worry about the extent to which research is inhibited by the presence of these narcissistic or highly critical parents and their ability to convince their children the fault lies with their own behavior rather than the parent. How much research is not done to protect the ego of the parent who would destroy their child's ego? How often is the person with ADHD the scapegoat of research just as they are often a scapegoat to the highly critical parent?

I would be interested to see the administration and results of a scale measuring the complex trauma symptoms and response of individuals seeking assessment for ADHD, especially in adulthood. It might be possible to use something like the Childhood Trauma Questionnaire, which is a screening tool used in adults to assess childhood maltreatment [77], or a similar assessment to the Intimate Violence and Traumatic

Affects Scale (VITA Scale) [78], even if these tools are not used to show direct cause but to open the door to additional study by showing a high enough correlation. The damage of CPTSD is so severe that even healing with a parent might not be enough to overcome the symptoms. And the symptoms of ADHD are so pervasive that an apology will not really be enough to heal it, either.

Sometimes it is the system that has been established (think back to the triangle of trauma) that hinders a person from growth in this healing. The triangle of trauma identifies a third role that can often influence CPTSD and is difficult to identify due to protective factors in the mind of the survivor. Often the unhelping bystander is the person or parent who is not the abusive one, but also does not save the child from the abuse. When they are ready, it has been helpful for clients in the past to see this person as more of a friendly henchman to an abuser. They are kind and make life a little bit easier while also playing their part in the system.

This position is also called the rescuer. Unfortunately, they are doomed to fail in their attempt to rescue due to the system of abuse that has been developed. We can often see this type of system set up in cults where abusers are protected. Survivors are punished for wanting help while the rescuer is shunned or cast out as a reminder to the survivor to not pull others into the process and disrupt the secrecy of the abuse. These tertiary roles in trauma are often the most difficult to recognize after how kindly this person treated the survivor, which can place guilt and blame on the survivor.

I consider guilt and shame as anger that is not allowed to be felt toward someone else and is thus turned inward on ourselves. Survivors of CPTSD can feel guilt for anger toward this person who refuses to save them. The guilt can also be derived from being trained that expressing anger toward a caretaker for their failure to care or propensity to abuse is not allowed in the family system. Survivors will learn that they can at least get their anger out on themselves and are further treated with guilt and shame by the system for this action to a point it also becomes internalized. So how can we heal from this?

Part VI: Healing

Chapter 21
Mindfulness

 Mindfulness is a strange and often overcomplicated thing that is at its foundation intentionally paying attention. As a practice, it has been commandeered by pseudo-experts and twisted into something much more complicated and abstract than it really is. This gatekeeping pushes people away, which is exactly what happened to me for many years. However, I have learned that it really is as simple as paying attention to one specific thing or many things all around you at once. Mindfulness can be accomplished through many roles that we play in life, if we can let "be" all that is witnessed. It's not the intent to change or to ponder.

 I took a class on mindfulness in grad school and was fearful that it would be some hippie dippie annoyance in my life having to listen to people preach about this or that and theories about the world that don't impact my world. I feared I would be slowed down by what could be a waste of my time. However, I learned in this class that many of my coping skills were mindfulness. I was told that I was a very mindful person despite these internal judgements toward what I was practicing.

 For example, there was a hill everyone would have to walk up to get into the school. I would often become out of breath in this process, and, I would learn, many others did as well. I used to pay attention to my shoes as I would walk up the hill as a distraction from my self-consciousness about being out of shape and unable to climb the hill without effort. I always slipped my shoes on instead of tying them each time. This left them slightly loose. In the walks up the hill I would begin to focus on the sensation of the shoe rocking back and forth on my foot in a slightly delayed cadence from my step. I would then focus harder and notice the difference between my foot and my shoe. I then would see if I could find the difference between my foot and my sock.

The mindfulness was in noticing these differences and experiencing them instead of focusing on my breath. Focusing on the breath is a common starting place for mindfulness, but for me, my breath was almost a trigger in those early days. It was difficult to pay attention to due to the internal judgment. I apparently often catch a short breath, which causes a slight panic in my body as if it's not receiving enough air. When I witness this, my mind decides to call myself an idiot who can't even breathe right. That was not where I could start learning the process of mindfulness despite all early meditations focusing so much on the breath. The breath was a trigger for my self-deprecating thoughts. It was not a safe space in which to exist. Instead, I used a trick I learned to focus on the physical sensation of cool air entering my nostrils rather than to focus on the breath. Later I was able to hover my hand outside of my body to telegraph the movement of the air and the depth in my lungs.

At first, paying attention can be painful due to one potentially toxic aspect of the mind: "the thinker." In his *Here and Now* series, Ram Dass discusses a meditation of when he sought to fast, but hunger kept him from separating from his earthly needs [79]. One day, he was able to find this separation during a meditation in which he was systematically disconnected from identifying as each part of his body, stating that he was not this part or that part, one at a time. The final line in the meditation was "I am not this thought." In response to this, I believe most people, including Ram Dass, start to think, "If I am not this thought, then who am I, and who said that?" The conclusion tends to be that the thinker is the one who says the thought and the witness is the one who hears it. We are both, and we can become more identified as the thinker when we are truly more of the witness.

Truly in our brains we are all of it. We are the wall on which the images are cast. We are the critics who sit and judge what passes by. We are the witnesses who hear the critics' judgements. We are the theater in which the movie is showing. We are all these roles, and we are none of these roles at the same time. We are not even truly separate from the rest of the universe. Everything is one.

I remember sitting in a philosophy class as everyone was trying to conceptualize Spinoza's form of God and struggling so much. God was described as being everything and everything being made of it, rather than an individual, personified deity. It made sense to me that to conceptualize this would be easy as a circle. The line between me and the rest of the universe never breaks. It would be like the horizon and the skyline being one in a silhouette. The silhouette is all one and unbroken when the shadow joins them, and yet we know there is individuality in those shapes. This is nonduality.

Nonduality is a concept in mindfulness that seems to trip up a lot of people. Everything and all are one; there is no true separation. The universe is drawn on an Etch A Sketch with the line never actually breaking, and yet we are all separate with no molecule touching another, merely vibrating closely together to form shape and matter. I believe nonduality is in that matter and energy are one and not separate in the way we label them. When considered this way, everything is connected, from matter to energy and energy to matter through the infinite universe. Mindfulness and nonduality is not the intellectual concept that we are all connected but rather attempting to feel that connection with the universe through meditation and intentionally paying attention.

Mindfulness is often a guide toward acceptance of all, or what is called radical acceptance. Tara Brach brought the idea into mindfulness while Marsha Linehan coined the term in her development of Dialectical Behavioral Therapy (DBT) [80]. I had come to this conclusion through my own work in mindfulness when I realized that the only control we truly have in this world is to give up the illusion that we have any control at all. Radical acceptance is not even that radical when you think about it. If the control you have is an illusion, then the only way to have any control is to accept that you have none rather than wasting energy exerting force on what may never change. Alcoholics Anonymous has another way of stating this in the serenity prayer [81]: "God grant me the serenity to accept the things I cannot change, the strength to change the things I can, and the wisdom to know the difference."

Another famous name in the world of mindfulness is that of Jon Kabat-Zinn. He is the founder of Mindfulness Based Stress Reduction (MBSR). MBSR is the CBT of mindfulness and is so well manualized that its effects are repeatable and able to be scientifically studied. Many of the studies on mindfulness have come out of these practices brought to the western world through Kabat-Zinn's MBSR, developed after he had attended a speaking engagement with a Buddhist monk in 1979 at MIT [82]. Mindfulness is the adapted form of Buddhism in a more digestible form for us Americans who might not have the time or discipline to devote to enlightenment while trying to exist in a capitalist hellscape.

In this video, Kabat-Zinn gives a talk at Dartmouth College on mindfulness and tells the story of finding mindfulness [82]. He describes so perfectly the idea of dropping in on yourself with the simple use of a tennis ball, demonstrating mindfulness in a truly straightforward way. He further discusses the aspect of the here and now and how things have turned out from when we used to plan for the future. We are not in the future or the past, we are here now, and this is what we have. I tend to refer my clients who are interested in mindfulness to this video due to all that it covers.

These philosophical ideas are not all mindfulness can encompass. Niazi and Niazi (2011) also discuss the physical benefits of mindfulness in the body managing disease and other health factors [83]. This is not a cure-all for disease, but it can provide a benefit alongside medical treatment. Beyond psychological issues such as depression or anxiety, it can help to manage chronic pain, hypertension, skin disorders, and immune disorders. MBSR has also shown changes in immune system markers for patients with cancer following an eight-week MBSR program [83].

Kabat-Zinn also discusses the effect of mindfulness on telomeres, which I had touched on earlier. Alda et al. (2016) shows that mindfulness indeed lengthens telomeres but is unable to answer why. They posit that it might have something to do with acceptance, which they measure through the absence of experiential avoidance with the second version of the Acceptance and Action Questionnaire (AAQ-II) [84]. This would make sense, as much of mindfulness is about the observation and acceptance of the world rather than attempts or desires to change it.

The desire to change something that cannot change can be a great cause of stress. Radical acceptance in this way manages the stress of the uncontrollable. Coming back to my grad school experience, the classroom in which I learned more about mindfulness had a door that made a squeaking noise as it rattled, and a dog outside was always barking. I would say this was a perfect place to learn mindfulness due to the limitations of control on the environment. We did eventually make changes to have more control, but the first day we had to learn to accept what could not be changed at the time.

At this time in my life, I was able to conquer insomnia, and the symptoms of my ADHD (which I didn't know were ADHD yet) had settled into manageable and, dare I say, peaceful times. My experience with mindfulness in as little as 30 minutes and a short reflection paper each week (the required assignment) led to me feeling what people often describe in social media when they take a stimulant for the first time after diagnosis. I felt calm, peace, and silence for possibly the first time in my life. My head was a safe space and all I had to do was find acceptance. This is not the case today, due to the pandemic and the chaos of life that flowed in during that time, and I need to get back there. However, mindfulness was the best coping skill I have ever had, and at the time it cured the two worst things in my life: my never-stopping brain and insomnia.

It would also make sense based on the Grant study mentioned in Chapter 10, where stress was seen to be a high indicator of reduced life expectancy and enjoyment [32]. Mindfulness and the acceptance that comes with practice can reduce this stress. The reduction in stress might lead to lengthening in telomeres and actually increase quality of life. I sometimes note that a monk in prison is not imprisoned due to the freedom of their mind. Acceptance and expansion of the mind can free a person from torment at least for a time, and it is like a muscle and can be honed.

Earlier I had discussed cannabis as a maladaptive coping skill for ADHD, as it can help to change the perception of time. Mindfulness is also capable of doing this. Through well-practiced mindfulness, a person can make time move faster or slower depending on the engagement with the world and their mind. Our minds are powerful things; during extreme fear the world can slow to a standstill, and with intense pleasure the world moves so quickly we nearly miss it. Mindfulness can give us the ability to manage this skill in our minds and move through torment faster while remaining in pleasure longer. Mindful eating is an example of the latter.

Is it harder for people with ADHD to meditate? Possibly, at first. Our assignment in the mindfulness class was 30 minutes of mindfulness per week. The teacher preferred we do it in a single sitting, but we were allowed to do it in increments, too. I had to do increments, as my brain could not sit still for more than 30 seconds at first, let alone 30 minutes. I started with 30 seconds to a minute. I would engage in sensory exploration during these times. Getting to three minutes in this way was less difficult. I specifically would press my face against the wall of the shower and try to distinguish between the hot water and the colder condensed water on the wall. It was strange to feel both at the same time.

The heater in my car was also broken during this semester of school, and it was winter. I would drive to school in the morning, and instead of feeling cold, I would explore what the word cold meant and try to feel the individual aspects that made up cold. It's funny how my brain, while exploring the meaning of the word cold, took away the form of avoidance that would often scream in my head to find a way to warm up or want to get away from the cold at all costs. Just changing my perspective to one of curiosity removed the torment of the experience and changed my overall sense of being. It was also an effective way to distract myself through the commute time.

Caution: be careful anytime you are trying to perform mindfulness while driving. While I was aware of everything around me and not just focused on the cold while doing this, it might not have been the safest choice.

Mindfulness is like a muscle. Building it makes it easier, and even people with ADHD can strengthen this muscle quite a bit. I would say that mindfulness is likely one of the best coping mechanisms for ADHD and managing the symptoms despite the high learning curve in building said muscle. It is best to build the tolerance for mindfulness with things you enjoy or might have enjoyed as a kid. Running my hand through the rain droplets on a metal slide as a kid comes to mind, as does kicking leaves in the fall during a mindful walk. Work up to the process of meditation by developing more coping skills to tolerate sitting still. In fact, a study by Kim et al. (2022) showed improvements in outcomes with ADHD and ego identity when scored. They define ego identity as "the sense of self to experience who they are" [85].

Distress tolerance is an important part of DBT and mindfulness. It can help you learn to adapt and develop new coping skills due to the discomfort. Most of humanity grows under the pressure of discomfort, as long as it is not to a level that is crushing. If sitting still with yourself is difficult for 45 seconds, see if you can push past a minute without harming yourself and making mindfulness a negative experience. Explore the emotions of discomfort and boredom. What do they feel like? How do you differentiate between them? What is the progressive development of emotion from start to intolerable? Explore how your mind handles these issues, and it can benefit with increasing tolerance and developing new coping skills.

Any person can engage in some form of mindfulness no matter their lifestyle.

Chapter 22

Boundaries

Boundaries are one of the most important coping skills in managing the relationship with a difficult person, let alone a narcissist or boundary-resistant person. They are a way of creating a healthy and safe relationship with even the most harmful people. That does not mean difficult people will adhere to any boundary, but the natural anger of a violated boundary will often encourage you to distance yourself from or even terminate the relationship. Without boundaries, resentment builds into hate and then into apathy if allowed to go that far. Why would you ever want to hate someone you care about? Boundary setting can be simple once you learn how to do it.

I have three simple rules in setting boundaries with other people. Let us call them the three Cs of boundaries: consideration, consent, and capacity. (I couldn't figure out how to make them Bs or that might have been catchier.) I pulled these rules from some of the requirements of contract law. A boundary is just an emotional contract. It says what is and what is not okay for each party of the agreement. To start, we need consideration, or, in other words, the expectation of a need to be met. Second is consent. Everyone must agree. Third is capacity. Some people will agree to anything, and we need to make sure they can deliver what is promised. Let me break each C down further.

Consideration starts with the expectation of a need to be met. We expect things daily, and many of these expectations are built into society. Boundary setting comes in when we might need something outside of the norm or when for whatever reason what we need is not available to us. You can't get angry at someone for not giving you something you never asked for. This would be without consideration. That just simply is not fair (except in the case of infants). If you have an expectation, you must communicate it clearly and ensure you are heard, but this is not a guarantee that your expectations will be met.

Consent is the agreement piece of any boundary. Just because you have an expectation doesn't mean I have any requirement of meeting it (unless legally you do as a parent). Both parties must agree to the expectation to be met. This is also the phase where negotiations would happen. You are allowed to say no. People are also allowed to walk away from relationships if the need is great enough and answered with a no, or the request is too great, and you have to say no. The final consequence for a boundary not being met is the end of a relationship, but it should rarely end up in this space. All or nothing is not boundary setting. That is an ultimatum and oppressing power in a relationship.

Finally, capacity is the ability of a person to meet the need they agreed to. Some people will agree to anything even if they are not capable and sometimes when they have no plan to meet said need despite agreeing. This is not the mob. You should not be breaking people's legs when they cannot or will not meet your emotional needs. Walking away is always an option. Capacity is also the catch-all to make sure we don't blame the other person completely. The adage of "fool me once shame on you, fool me twice shame on me" fits here. A person who continues to allow others to walk all over them can't blame the people they keep giving this power to. We either move the bar, remove the expectation, or walk away.

Boundaries keep us safe. We know when a person is jumping up and down excitedly that it might not be a smart idea to stand six inches away from them. This is a case where distance provides protection. A person who calls us and makes us feel poorly after every call might need to have a call or two skipped until healthier boundaries can be put in place. The goal is safety. What do you need to be safe? Boundaries also ensure we are not in pain or hate and can continue to love others. No one can decide what you need other than you, but they can suggest options for consideration.

I can't remember where I heard it, but I once heard someone say that he keeps people at a distance where he can still love them. That statement was profound. We do not need to hate anyone in life other than those who do not respect the space we need to continue to love them. Some people might be great and yet rub you the wrong way. A cashier at a grocery store can be nice and not want to date a person they are nice to. Maybe that one coworker is good at their job, but you don't have a good personal relationship with them. In most cases, people who hurt or anger you don't have to be allowed to have access to you. This of course is not meant to describe situations where abusers won't allow this to happen or utilize the courts to force closeness.

We can set some boundaries to achieve these needs assuming the person is not malicious. When someone says something that hurts you, you don't have to convince them. You are allowed to distance yourself for a time until you are able to build up communication and boundary setting skills to have a constructive discussion and keep them in your life. This is the purpose of no contact where possible. Going no contact can help you strengthen your skills to be able to stand up to people and ask for what you need. Staying no contact is often up to the person who you are requesting boundaries from.

If you're on the phone with a parent and they mention something painful that you don't want to discuss, you can ask them to stop. When they don't stop or bring it up five minutes later, you can tell them you have to go. You are not required to tell them why, and they don't have to agree with you. After a time of acting out, they will start to respect the boundary, even if it is out of frustration of its existence. Or they won't, and you don't have to talk to them. You do not have to save them when they play the victim of "I'm sorry I was a bad parent." You do not need to respond at all to these statements.

Tony Overbay of the Virtual Couch Podcast [86] has a video on TikTok about the popcorn method in dealing with these narcissistic parents in a moment. They describe an interaction between a narcissistic parent and a person eating popcorn. Each time the narcissistic parent looks for the adult child to give them a reprieve or save them emotionally, the person does not respond for the amount of time it takes to imagine eating a piece of popcorn. This leads to the narcissistic parent shifting from blaming, to the martyr, to frustration, to rage, and finally hanging up [87]. This behavior of looking for a specific response is the reason people with ADHD are often targeted by narcissists. If we care about the narcissist and have to be around them, we tend to fawn to their emotional needs. If we do not have to deal with them or do not know them, we might ignore their attempts to engage looking for performative emotion.

Performative emotion is fawning. Some people try to make us laugh or smile. That can be nice, except when you do not laugh or smile and they become angry. This is a case of performative emotion and is not a request. Men will often do this when they tell women to smile more. Why? They didn't say "be happy more." They are commanding people to put on masks. I have ADHD and struggle in the mornings to talk to people until I have a chance to get to where I am going and sit down. People sometimes have a huge problem with this and accuse me of ignoring them. I heard you; I just don't have the emotional space for you right now.

Some people will back up when you confront their behavior and say, "I was only asking a question." That's fine. In fact, one of my strongest boundaries starts with this. People will sometimes ask if they can ask me personal questions as their therapist. I tell everyone the same thing: "You can ask as long as I'm allowed to say no." If you are not allowed to say no, they are not really asking. That earns an automatic "no" from me. Their expectation can be that I respond to them. I disagree. The relationship progresses no further. Or they express the expectation, I explain myself and what I can offer, and they accept or reject said offer. This is a bit confrontational, but remember that you do not owe someone the right to harm you.

Other people would often tell me my expectations were unfair or their expectations were only common sense. If you do not tell someone your expectation, they are not beholden to it. Common sense is just a tricky way of expressing my expectations. Common sense is not what it seems. The same lessons are not inherent to everyone. Mostly, people would use common sense defense to pressure me into doing what they wanted. However, common sense is different in every culture. So common sense defense is based on privilege of expecting someone to follow your culture over their own. Assume no boundary is common sense and communicate yours to others with compassionate yet assertive language the first time.

Sometimes we might need to go above assertive language and not toe the line of compassion as the boundary violation becomes emergent. Our language needs to also convey the appropriate level of response to the violation. This is not to say you should yell at everyone who angers you or pushes a boundary. Instead, meet the need of the moment. A person about to run off a cliff might need to be yelled at due to the urgency of the need. A person threatening you might need to be handled in a separate way still. However, a person asking for the time does not deserve to be screamed at. Emergent needs (or needs that feel like an emergency to meet in the moment) can also seem to arise out of nowhere.

Sometimes when we forget or can't express our boundaries or needs, those needs become so great it feels like we might explode. These are times when our expression of need is out of line with what might be expected by others. Many might see this as irrational behavior due to not knowing what is going on inside a person's own mind or body. Interoception is the system by which we notice and address the physical and emotional state of the body. Think of a time when you might have been doing something and suddenly felt the need to urinate to the point of emergency. This might be due to poor interoception. Neurodivergent people often have poor interoception and can have emotional outbursts due to emergent emotional needs that were under the surface unnoticed until they were too much.

We can even set boundaries with ourselves to notice when certain thresholds are crossed, as trying to be aware 24/7 of all our needs might be unrealistic and fall into the area of capacity. Let us call them check points: areas that approach problematic feelings that have led to outbursts in the past. If an interaction feels awkward with a friend, it might be an innovative idea to do what therapy calls "bringing it into the room." Let's talk about the awkwardness with our friend and our desire to handle difficult emotions, if necessary, rather than be surprised by them later. This can be an exceedingly tricky thing to do. It won't mean the emotions won't come, but you might be more prepared to feel them without entering a state of panic. I notice my own tendencies in ADHD can trigger others who have trauma with narcissism and will sometimes discuss this when I notice someone shift emotionally and suspect that as a reason.

The basis of boundaries is that to maintain any relationship, I don't want to hurt you, and you should not want to hurt me. Beyond that, if those statements are true, nothing is off the table for discussion because it's not personal. So many couple sessions have been poor due to past resentments and fear of future harm until we realize that everyone in that room is there to heal. The sessions gain a vastly different tone when we realize the pain was coming as a reaction to old pain and even the person having those reactions would be happier not to have them. It can be a beautiful thing to watch two people interact in a feeling of safety with one another rather than fear and retribution.

Some people will not respect boundaries despite them telling you otherwise. This can be due to choice or unavoidable due to capacity. People in either situation can only be given so many chances to fail before we take their capacity into consideration to protect ourselves from the pain. This is the ability that we often don't have as a child when the parent or adult in power is the one breaking these boundaries. It is important to set the boundaries you can while remaining safe. I know not everyone is independent of their abusers. People who are unhealthy are often the people who repeatedly violate boundaries. This is not to say all people, but the people who are not genuine in seeking for their needs to be met often violate boundary after boundary.

In an analogous way, ADHD and the impulsivity of behaviors can often violate the boundaries of others due to that issue of capacity. You might not be able to change it, but if someone has a sunburn and you keep forgetting and slapping them on the back, you should stand outside of your arms' reach for a while. However, understand some people might not be able to forgive these limitations of forgetfulness and impulsivity. That is their right to protect themselves, even if it is not our fault intentionally. We do not expect people to eat food if they are allergic to it just because we spent time making it for them without knowing. Both can be true at the same time. We don't want to pressure people to be uncomfortable when they don't have to be.

Chapter 23
Autonomy

The idea of Autonomy is discussed in Erik Erikson's psychosocial development stages [88]. Autonomy is the ability to govern and manage ourselves in a way that can be trusted by those around us. During our second stage of development (about 1-3 years old), we hope to overcome shame and doubt in the strengthening of autonomy to develop our will. This is often the stage in which "helicopter parenting" can inhibit our ability to trust ourselves and limit the development of our self-efficacy with internalized doubt from external sources. Toddlers are tiny scientists interacting with the world which has real consequences. The more successful the toddler, the more autonomous they may become later in life.

Autonomy is also the ability to take care of ourselves without oversight. Why is life harder with ADHD? It can often be difficult to engage in self-care and basic needs around hygiene when our systems are disrupted, such as happened during the lockdown of 2020. Increased stress breaks down the energy we need to maintain the system while also living within said system. Decreases in cleanliness and increases in symptoms like forgetfulness and nesting can make a person seem off their hinges despite functioning in a system of chaos. This is the trick. Our environment might deteriorate, but we continue to thrive while devoting resources to other things that are important for the long term rather than organization when you can remember where in the mess everything is.

The problem with these areas of chaos in the life of a person with ADHD is that it can lead to a temporary loss in sense of self. Chaotic productivity takes its toll on a person and pushes them further into survival mode. Perhaps this is why the nesting behavior can look animalistic, like a den in the wild packed with comfortable materials. As a person fades into the fight or flight response, their emotional awareness lessens and numbs. Their recognition of being tired or worn out and needing self-care falls off, and they enter a pattern of diminishing returns. It is also during this time they become more susceptible to addiction and addictive behaviors.

All of this is not to say that people with ADHD do not function. They actually function very well despite basically captaining a sinking ship. People with ADHD are incredibly gifted in the ability to redirect focus and resources. They tend to be able to make extraordinarily little last much longer than it should through desperation and ingenuity. In a human-centered design engineering work group, they are the hurdler or the problem solver. They are also skilled at managing crises and are labeled as the performer during these times. However, they seem unhinged if you look at their deteriorating self-care routines.

So, the answer to whether or not they lack a sense of self often comes down to how safe and structured their life feels and whether they have access to their emotions or feel numb right now. These scales could likely tell you the emotional health of a person with ADHD despite any crisis going on. It can lead to another question: Do people with ADHD struggle with self-care? Yes, especially when they are in some form of crisis or routines have broken down. People with ADHD can often feel numb while things are getting worse. It is almost how our brain works with pain during extreme situations to numb it until we are calm and safe enough to handle it. You don't realize how wounded you are until you have time to look at it—and then it starts hurting. With ADHD, the problem is often that a person feels so uncomfortable in that calm setting that they look for reasons to not be there (or look at it).

A person with ADHD can struggle to engage in self-care due to finding too many other things that must be done first, which might *technically* be true. These tasks allow a person to not recognize the state they are in and continue to function despite it. However, if they can't notice the level to which their mental health and emotional state has deteriorated, they will not be able to implement self-care to correct for the need. This becomes the endless cycle of being too tired to function and too busy to sleep. Something will break eventually if self-care does not happen by choice. The body and mind will shut down in a way to make it happen by force.

The extreme nature of ADHD leads to it being diagnosed and treated as a disability. This is especially true when it meets these levels of dysfunction. I will discuss the implications of it as a disability in the next chapter. But I want to make clear around autonomy that ADHD can become so disorganized that a person would meet the criteria of disability under the Americans with Disabilities Act. Considering this, the government has done one cordial thing for people with ADHD (a disability): People with ADHD can get a National Parks pass for free. This would provide immense self-care if there were not so many roadblocks to getting it.

People with ADHD have a propensity to isolate themselves when stressed, which can interfere with their self-care ability and wellness monitoring from support systems. Do people with ADHD like to be alone? They sure think they do, whether or not that is an effective treatment for their burnout. This can be a danger to the mind of a person with ADHD, as it can promote rumination and racing thoughts. A person alone is never challenged in their thought process and therefore is in danger of believing everything they produce, which can exacerbate any comorbid symptoms of depression or anxiety. Being alone is not great for people with ADHD for periods greater than 48 to 72 hours without any human contact (I might have made this number up).

Being alone is not great for anyone who's experienced trauma, or for humanity as a whole. One recent study suggests a link between social isolation and the increase in psychotic symptoms [89]. This would make sense, as we had seen in earlier studies a link to psychotic symptoms increases and torture. The psychological coercive environmental factor specifically identifies isolation as an example in this study [90].

People with ADHD have found a way to avoid the torture of the internalized highly critical voice in their heads through avoidance. You could almost equate this response to the image of "psychotic or paranoid" characters in movies desperately searching piles of newspapers for evidence to prove they are not crazy. There is a reason movies and television depict mentally unwell people in this way. To some degree it can be accurate; as a person deteriorates mentally, their environment and outward appearance become more unkempt. A lack of showering and growing a beard were signs of encroaching psychosis in older movies.

The messiness and organizational behaviors of a person with ADHD are not always related to being mentally unwell. They might be related to neurodivergent behaviors and thoughts, but that is different from unwell. Earlier I had discussed that something must inhibit areas of your life to a certain threshold before the symptoms can be considered disordered. Many of the neurodivergent behaviors discussed among people who are neurodivergent don't even make it into the DSM criteria for ADHD. This can include things such as pathological demand avoidance or rejection sensitivity dysphoria. ADHD is also a cognitive processing disorder despite it often being characterized as hyperactivity, lack of focus, and impulsivity.

It can be the opposite of all these issues. A person with ADHD can be hyperactive, or they might be paralyzed by fear and avoidance of a task while doing nothing all day due to needing to complete one specific task, a form of executive dysfunction. They might also have incredible focus, referred to as hyperfocus, that drains their energy at an increased rate compared to neurotypicals. They can even be very deliberate in their actions counter to the idea of impulsivity in tasks such as doing the laundry or cleaning up their bedroom. A person with ADHD does not avoid these chores out of laziness. They avoid them out of a distorted thought process due to a cognitive processing disorder.

Why does a person with ADHD struggle with the laundry or have a messy bedroom? To the average person doing the laundry might be three steps:

1. Wash
2. Dry
3. Fold

Doing the laundry is anywhere from upwards of 30-50 steps for a person with ADHD (the below example is only a small taste):

1. Go to the bedroom and grab the laundry.
2. Decide whether to sort clothing into lights and darks before getting frustrated and throwing it all in at once.
3. Realize it has been too long and all of it does not fit in the machine anymore.
4. Set the first load to wash.
5. Decide what to add since fabric softener is bad now and white vinegar is good.

6. Think about the smell of vinegar for a while and hesitate on starting the load.
7. Put in the soap and start the load.
8. Wander away and forget about the laundry.
9. Remember the laundry and go switch it to the dryer while having the same previous conversations in your head with the rest of the load that would not fit earlier.
10. Get both the washing machine and the dryer going.
11. Wander away to do something else for an hour.
12. Forget that you were doing laundry.
13. Finally remember there was laundry in the machines.
14. Take out the dry clothes and throw them in a basket.
15. Transfer the wash to the dryer and start the dryer.
16. Take the basket of dry clothes to where they might be put away to fold them with the plan of doing so when the other load finishes.
17. Forget the other load in the dryer . . . for a few days and avoid the pile of laundry that was done and needed folded in the bedroom.
18. Realize the clothes are wrinkled and the drying process must be done again.

Did you read all the steps or skim them? Was it overwhelming? Did you just want it to end? Me too. That nightmare is the reason I cannot complete laundry and would often pay people to do it for me. Luckily, I was able to trade chores with my wife so that I would not be responsible for the laundry. I am also a hot-blooded person, and folding warm clothes makes me sweat. It is a very unpleasant experience and takes so much mental energy to complete each time. At one point in my life, I had even bought enough clothes to wear daily and not be forced to do laundry for at least a month. People with ADHD also have issues with object permanence. Setting something down or walking away and forgetting something is happening will lead to completely forgetting the thing ever existed until some stimulus reminds you.

This can also often be an issue for autonomy in jobs. People with ADHD are great at getting a ton of work done quickly with minor mistakes. The opposite can also be true with them being detail oriented and focusing so hard on details that it saps their brain power for the rest of the day or week. The importance here is utilizing your employees well. Micromanaging someone with ADHD will only frustrate you and them. A person with ADHD does not work the same way a neurotypical person works, and those expectations are, as I will discuss in the next chapter, discriminatory, even if agreed to, due to capacity.

Chapter 24
Discrimination

Discrimination is a difficult subject which can make anyone feel defensive. I don't mean the people with disabilities, rather those without. For some reason, many people perceive reasonable accommodations as unfair advantages even when these "advantages" do not affect that person's ability to compete in competitive settings. I remember seeing it reflected in the story of Casey Martin when he was suing the PGA for the right to use a golf cart during competition due to a circulatory issue that affected his legs. He was forced to take it to the Supreme Court to be granted his rights, even though golfers said they had no problem with it and enjoyed walking.

It seems ironic that people who are not suffering from something that limits them look at people with a disability with envy. I talk to clients about envy around these subjects often. Sometimes it can be as simple as the benefits afforded a sibling or someone else around them. Other times it might be the relationships they have access to. The one question that always cancels this cognitive dissonance, if they are able to deconstruct it, is, "Do you want to live their life with all of their difficulty and experience exactly as they have had to live it?" If the answer is not simply a "yes," then you do not want their accommodation bad enough.

It is not fair to look at others who are struggling and think, "I want what they are getting but without all the bad parts." Who are you? It's giving the bully on the playground playing around with the crutches of a person with a broken bone and refusing to give them back because "they're fun." I know some people struggle with seeing others be accommodated due to their own internal pain of having to struggle without acknowledgement. However, we don't need to fight over validation. It is limitless and free. You gaining something does not make me lose it, or at least it shouldn't be handled or perceived that way.

Sometimes workplaces and society might make coworkers of someone with a disability notice the advantages of the accommodation and develop a retaliatory response without evidence of such. The third role of the triangle of trauma comes out in this way. The unhelping bystander becomes the enforcer. I have played the role of enforcer before, and I feel shame for doing so. I worked at a place that had a heavy workload, and when someone called out, that workload was put on another employee. That other employee was often me because of how little I called out, which was related to shame from childhood over sick days. I would pressure people near me not to take mental health days due to the work that was placed on me and the minimal effect it seemed to have for those colleagues.

This was absolutely wrong. I was playing the enforcer of the system to get the other abused employees to take their hits rather than asking why this system forces so many to suffer. The enforcer role is often a way for workplace discrimination to not reach an actionable level as it would be nearly impossible to prove. Do not think just because it cannot reach the level of legal liability that it is not abusive. This chapter discusses discrimination in a way that looks at the pain it can cause and the limits of support, or limitations in life.

I am not using the legal burden of proof when discussing discrimination. I am moreso using a definition that would include less apparent forms of discrimination and retaliation including microaggressions. Whether these forms of discrimination are intentional or unintentional isn't important in this discussion. The effects of microaggressions and discrimination are also true about other traumatic things in life. It would be easier to just ignore it rather than start a fight to set a boundary. This should not be the case nowadays, where a person asking for help is then further abused for daring to question the generosity of others. That's messed up.

That is also one great issue with asking for reasonable accommodation or even mentioning that you have a disability. It could lead to a file being opened on you and for the collection of data to monitor you closer than your colleagues in case they must get rid of you without having a federal case made of the issue. This is discriminatory by virtue if not by law. Oppressive people often get uncomfortable around the idea of people advocating for their rights. It makes sense. They should be uncomfortable. That is their conscience telling them it is wrong.

The image above [Deposit Photos] is such a good depiction of the use of equity and justice in the world of discrimination. Many workplaces will provide equality and call it equity or unreasonable accommodation. Equity gives those with some form of disability the chance to achieve the same as a person without the disability. These needs for equity are directly due to the structures and norms of the environment. Justice looks to remove those barriers that would require equity in the first place. However, justice is often more difficult to provide, especially when a company has no desire to make changes and does not see the issue as a disability that deserves accommodation.

Is ADHD a disability? Yes, it is considered a disability and is protected under the ADA. It can be referred to as an invisible disability. This is due to the symptoms of ADHD not often being seen as symptoms but rather as personality or moral characteristics. Laziness is one of the most common descriptions of ADHD by those who have not experienced it. However, as described in earlier chapters, ADHD is amazing in a crisis scenario. But this might also mean that they are terrible when things are mundane and there are little to no deadlines. Self-management of deadlines is difficult for me.

Invisible disabilities often get labeled as something other than what they are. ADHD is commonly called laziness, and the use of medication is often discouraged by authority figures practicing beyond their scope. All I ever heard about ADHD as a child was how these kids are faking it, and they just need to buckle down and try harder. The parents of Millennials were often Baby Boomers. These Baby Boomers had a higher level of narcissism in part due to lead poisoning that caused brain damage [91]. If my idea that narcissism is a leading factor in the development of ADHD, it would explain why Millennials were specifically diagnosed at what seemed like a higher rate from the 1980s through the 1990s and into their school ages of the early 2000s.

Laziness feels more like a lazy explanation to distance responsibility from parenting methods. This era also included the latchkey kids, who have been studied for the effects of neglect on children and the persistence of these effects into adulthood. Children were expected to take care of themselves often without coaching in ways of soothing. The "cry it out" method was a good excuse for neglect when it was not performed in the way it was intended for sleep training. Children are the ones without power in the family dynamic. They should not be the ones expected to develop the solutions to the failures of a system, just as any oppressed group should not be expected to fix the system that is harming them.

I have had many jobs in my life, which I now realize was likely due to undiagnosed ADHD. I would get a job and try to learn everything I could about it. I would then learn ways to improve my efforts and make my work more efficient. This was sometimes seen as a good thing. Some of my bosses saw my abilities to get stuff done as an asset and treated me that way. I excelled in these jobs. Some bosses would only see me when I was resting from doing what might have been three hours' worth of work in one hour and thought of me as lazy. These jobs often had microaggressions, neglect, retaliation, and accusations of laziness. My work effort reflected how my superiors saw me. I performed when I felt safe and secure and failed when I did not.

Jobs that had spurts of activity and crisis had always been the most fun to me. I was able to get lost in the work for a time through my hyperfocus. Jobs with lengthy periods of down time were not so great for me, as I would become less motivated when I had less to do. In my experience, micromanaging from employers often led to less work and less motivation. I could complete the list quickly, but they would look for flaws in my work. I could delay the list over the course of the workday, but that was torturous. My ADHD affords me a superpower if I am utilized effectively and a disability when I am not.

My colleagues think I do too much when I tell them my schedule and goals. I ran 12 groups a week in my internship and had a few individual clients, racking up about 30 notes to write per day. My first position for work was seeing 29 clients a week before taking on IOP and running many of those groups again at the same location, in addition to 15 clients per week. I had written over 10,000 notes by the time I left that job after three and a half years. The job after that had me running at least 10 groups a week with individual sessions for each client per week and a caseload of 16 people on average. The paperwork was immense due to the requirements of inpatient treatment. I was able to do it all. I burned out due to some abusive behaviors by management near the end of my stay at the last job around the three-year mark. There were also unsafe changes and questionable ethics used during the pandemic at that same time.

I felt like I would never be able to get back to doing as much work as I had done before. After about a year, I had a schedule that had 58 spots for 45-minute sessions with clients in individual work. That was a little too much, and I am down to around 37 spots now. I was working over 44 hours per week, thinking to myself that I could never go back to a 40-hour work week. All the while, I had been working far more than that for well over a year. My burnout was not the work that I love. It was the discrimination that I received at various levels of my career. Self-care also helps to prevent any form of burnout in what I love doing.

I say all this not to say that I am superhuman. I just do what I enjoy and take the responsibility that comes with it. I say this to let anyone with ADHD know that if you can find the right fit for your needs, you will be a rockstar in your field. Our minds work in such strange and unique ways that we see issues long before they happen. We build efficient systems that help those around us. We take pride in our work since our work needs to be fulfilling for us to stay engaged. ADHD can be a curse, but it can also allow us to make monumental changes to the world, especially for those with whom we share the disability moniker.

Part VII: Barriers

Chapter 25
Assessment

ADHD is a unique disorder to have and to have diagnosed. Due to the medical stimulants often prescribed for this disorder, many professionals and insurance companies will err on the side of caution in the process of diagnostics. This can sometimes lead to multiple professionals requiring retesting of the same individual due to the separation of multiple disciplines treating the same person. Assessment is often the gatekeeper for proper diagnosis and treatment. There are many barriers to this aspect of treatment alone including cost, availability, required credentials of the assessor, cost, insurance coverage, and inherent medical biases, to name a few—and don't forget cost.

Why is it so hard to get assessed for ADHD? That's a tricky question to answer, since it seems no one truly knows the depths of difficulty each person has to go through for their diagnosis. Insurance companies can credential and panel assessors, but this process takes time and money that many assessors are not willing to take. Since many assessors therefore don't take insurance, you can see an assessor and hope your insurance will cover the cost through out-of-network benefits. However, these are not guaranteed for each assessor or even each insurance plan. To use out-of-network coverage, the person seeking assessment will first have to pay out of pocket and hope for reimbursement. That is if they can even find an assessor with availability in the next six months and there are no changes to insurance coverage or financial stability in that time.

Beyond all of that, not every practitioner trusts that the previous practitioners had gone through the right channels and used the correct assessments. They can often request a person be retested due to their own disillusionment; they may think that ADHD is going away or is not bad enough to warrant a diagnosis or even that their exposure to ADHD is so great their diagnosis threshold is higher than clinically appropriate. Medical professionals typically do this because the prescribing of a scheduled substance is highly monitored due to the misuse of methamphetamines in rural areas of the United States. Whereas opioids are often the drug of choice in urban and suburban areas, meth is the drug of choice in rural areas due to the ease of making it at home and thus the increased access to these substances.

The reluctance to prescribe amphetamines could even be thought of as a form of medical discrimination, as these drugs are seen to be less than or cheaper than opioids and thus abused more often by people in poverty. These beliefs assign a moral superiority to opioid use due to its cost in pill form, much in the same way laws for crack cocaine criminalize it harsher than cocaine, which is typically more expensive. Essentially, the more expensive the drug, the less punishment assigned to the violation as a form of discrimination based on net worth. And so you can see the barrier to proper treatment is blocked with financial availability. A person is set to fail in being treated if they cannot afford the prohibitive cost of being assessed due to fear mongering and abuse of these substances by children of politicians, whom I will discuss later.

One of the major challenges of diagnosing ADHD in people is the fear of how they will react to the medication. Nonstimulants can take four to eight weeks to be effective before taking someone off them. Stimulants are instant in effectiveness if they are the right treatment. However, people without ADHD will respond poorly to these medications. Not to mention if a person has bipolar disorder the effect is mania. The cautionary tale against ease of diagnosis and prescription is often used as a warning of bad actors seeking substances. Abdelnour et al. (2022) looked at this issue and specifically noted that is not the case. This study specifically found that there was not an increase in feigning of symptoms in seeking medication with the increase in proper diagnosis [92].

This is like how moral superiority prevents the development of gambling through the belief more people will become gambling addicts. In Pennsylvania, state research has shown that the number of addicts remains consistent in proportion to the population of people gambling at around 3% [93]. Yale Medicine confirms similar numbers across the United States [94]. The number of left-handed people and people who identify as LGBTQIA+ has also increased due to factors other than some mad dash of conformity or abuse of the system benefits. I do not believe this to be a trend, but rather an increase in access to knowledge and a more accurate reflection of the actual population, especially since I was in denial despite two separate therapists telling me they thought I had ADHD. We need to stop treating ADHD diagnostics as a form of prevention in access to substances and instead the form of access to treatment for a genuine need.

Major and common barriers to assessment remain in the realm of cost and availability. An assessment for ADHD can range in required time from an hour or so up to ten hours at some practices. The price along with these assessments can range from around $500 to upwards of $10,000 and likely somewhere around the $2,500 mark. This is an expensive test, and many places have waiting lists that could delay decisions. In that time the cost can go up and the wait time can get longer. Waiting time can be anywhere from six months to multiple years.

This is especially problematic because people with ADHD have specific diagnostic criteria that affect their ability to follow through and make decisions.

I have seen this firsthand, as it is almost expected that a referral for someone with ADHD might take months to follow through just for the initial questionnaire to see if a diagnosis for ADHD is even worth pursuing. Speaking with colleagues, my clients have dropped off their communications during the decision-making process and avoided discussing ADHD in therapy. I am not exactly sure what the numbers are for referral to attrition, but I can guess they are high. In the addiction world, when someone calls for help, you go pick them up, as that window will close quickly. I believe something similar can happen with ADHD and the window of effort before the negative self-talk defeats it.

I have also seen the opposite happen where I talk to a client about getting tested for ADHD and they have a primary care physician who prescribes them a stimulant with no testing. In some cases, this turns out fine as the person reacts well to the medication, but in other instances this does not go as well, as people without ADHD respond to the medication as if it were meth. I do believe there needs to be a system in place to assess the diagnosis of this disorder due to the medication required to treat it, but that system cannot be discriminatory against the people who need it. There must be a balance in treating people without harming them through over- or undertreatment.

From my own experience and that of clients I've had who went through it, the assessment process is exceedingly difficult. The process takes a long time, and it is designed to frustrate someone with ADHD to the point that symptoms will start to show even if the person is adept at hiding them through coping skills. The process certainly affected me in this way. I was covered in sweat and looked like a mess following my assessment. The system of assessment is torturous in this way, as it will ask a person to focus on something and react in certain ways. A person with ADHD can be aware when they are running out of the ability to do these things and the number of failures along the way. This is not helpful to the need to be good enough and increases the negative self-talk and avoidant behaviors. It was not a fun experience, and if I had to wait six months to multiple years to complete said experience and pay multiple thousands of dollars, then I would have preferred to stay undiagnosed.

Two reasons not to follow through with diagnosis are due to medication and discrimination. The diagnosis is the barrier between being medicated and not. Medication can be helpful in treatment. However, as I will discuss in a future chapter, the Government/manufacturers have made production and distribution of this specific type of medication difficult, possibly to the point of causing shortages that did not exist before or *did* exist, were fixed, and then broken again by the Government/manufacturers. The second reason to get a diagnosis is to ask for reasonable accommodations at work for the disability of ADHD. This can be positive, or it can paint a target on your back for discrimination. Despite discrimination being illegal, it still happens every day.

Assessment is an incredibly high barrier to gaining a diagnosis that may lead to discrimination and the stigma as an addict at pharmacies, depending on who you must interact with. ADHD is often classified as laziness despite a diagnosis, and the world is not an accommodating place unless you end up in a chaotic environment and thrive. People do not often respect it as a disability. Monthly trips to a pharmacy for treatment often feel cumbersome to the point of not wanting to get the medication. You must fight to this point to get a pill that helps you remember to take your pill. And even if you do everything right, the job might determine you to be too much of a burden to continue to employ.

We need a new system of treatment and diagnosis.

Chapter 26
Medications

Medication seems to be the most controversial aspect of ADHD. There are a few medications that can be prescribed to treat this disorder. The main types of medications used to treat ADHD are stimulants, nonstimulants, and antidepressants. There are many stimulants used to treat ADHD, but the main prescription for adults these days is a variation of Adderall® or Vyvanse®. Nonstimulants include the drugs atomoxetine (Strattera®) and Qelbree™. Antidepressants often prescribed to treat ADHD comorbid with depression would be bupropion (such as Wellbutrin®) or possibly older forms of antidepressants called tricyclics. All these drugs require a prescription.

Stimulants increase activity in the brain. In the substance use world, they're known as uppers. Stimulant substances include caffeine, nicotine, cocaine, and meth. Stimulants help the brain to release dopamine, as mentioned in Chapter 16. Illicit drug versions of stimulants often release too much dopamine at once and lead to a negative response following the high. Medical versions of stimulants such as Adderall do not pass through the blood brain barrier like methamphetamines do and thus have a slightly different effect than the illicit drug. Think of stimulants as giving the prefrontal cortex or executive functioning center of the brain the energy to organize and run the thought process and task management of the body.

These stimulant medications' efficacy can also be affected by other aspects of the body, such as hormones or vitamins. Vitamin C has been known to inhibit the effect of stimulant medications in people with ADHD. Elevated levels of vitamin C can also remove the stimulant completely even after it has been absorbed. I have not heard this explained in the process of prescribing these medications, and many people with ADHD are shocked to hear it, though they note noticing a lesser effect on days they consumed something with vitamin C such as orange juice.

The issue of medication's efficacy in people assigned female at birth (AFAB) goes much beyond the easy fix of avoiding vitamin C. The menstrual cycle has fluctuations in hormones that have been found to affect the efficacy of medications, specifically in treating ADHD. One such study examined the use of a premenstrual dose elevation for stimulants and found this to be effective with no adverse events [95]. A major gap in treating ADHD for those with menstrual cycles has been missed for many years. Medications actually have not often been tested on people AFAB of childbearing age due to a change in FDA policy in the 1970's [96]. However, this does not explain why menstrual products were tested with saline instead of blood until a study in 2023 [97]. Or why we have only recently discovered toxic metals in tampons [98].

Nonstimulant medications work similarly to antidepressants in that they are reuptake inhibitors. Strattera is a norepinephrine reuptake inhibitor, and Qelbree is a dopamine reuptake inhibitor. These substances work by allowing the chemicals in your brain that are released between neurons in the synaptic gap more time to be absorbed by the receiving neuron. Thus, a deficit of the chemical forms in the firing neuron which then tells your brain to make more. The deficit effect of this can be why it takes four to eight weeks to start being effective.

Reuptake inhibitors are similar in function to antidepressants in this way, which is what the "RI" stands for in "SSRI."

Antidepressants are the third type of medication used in the treatment of ADHD. Wellbutrin specifically is often used due to the chemicals it acts on through its reuptake inhibitors. It is a norepinephrine and dopamine reuptake inhibitor (NDRI) and is often used with other ADHD medication, as the stimulant effect is usually compared to a cup of coffee. Like other medications, it can also take up to eight weeks to take full effect. This medication can be helpful to some, and others might hate it. This is true of any of these medications, as individual metabolism has a profound effect on the medication's efficacy.

In general, medication for psychiatric treatment can be spotty for some and perfect for others. Some medications take away all the undesired symptoms, while other medications might take away a mix of both good and distressing symptoms of ADHD. I can tell you that nonstimulant ADHD medication reduced issues with inattentive eating, strengthened my tolerance before getting frustrated, and allowed me to focus more without having to experience every moment of time. However, it also made me suffer if I acted as if I was still unmedicated, such as with poor sleep hygiene and lack of self-care. My body and mind would struggle to recover the next day, and tiredness could last weeks until I used coping skills to reduce this.

Another issue with the medication used in treating ADHD happens with more than just stimulant medications. Even the nonstimulant medications can be difficult to get filled at a pharmacy, as some of these medications are not commonly used as much as Adderall or Vyvanse. I was almost always running out of medication before the next refill was filled despite being prescribed. The withdrawal from nonstimulant medications felt for me like a brain fog with a constant headache that nothing would take away for the 48 hours after running out of my prescription until the 48 hours after taking it again. It was not fun.

I asked to stop taking these medications due to both this almost monthly withdrawal process and another side effect, increased blood pressure. This was also in addition to the medication being in capsules which float on water in your mouth and can hit the gag reflex. It did. Both pills. Every day. I loved some of the positive effects of the medication and having a nonstimulant gave me relief 24 hours a day if I had a prescription available for it. However, the lack of care in the psychiatric and pharmaceutical industry made me feel unsafe in my treatment, especially around holidays.

These issues can pale in comparison to the experience of those who have fought hard to have the right to take stimulant medications. These medications are almost always hard to find and in shortage since the intervention of the Government despite the release of 12 different generics for Vyvanse since the pandemic. Again, I will get to that in the next chapter. It is just so infuriating. These medications rarely last through the workday. Those pistachio commercials that would talk about the 2-3 pm lull in the workday seemed targeted at people with ADHD medicated by stimulants.

The stimulant tends to wear off around or just after lunch time, and some individuals need a secondary smaller dose to finish the workday. That's right. These medications are not prescribed to support people at home. They are used for focus in the workplace. That is unless you are lucky enough to be prescribed an extended-release version of the stimulant that will slowly release in your system for most of the day. Sometimes my clients with ADHD are also encouraged to not take their stimulant medication on the weekends.

None of these medications are perfect medications unless you happen to have the right luck. They all have their benefits and weaknesses, and the process to find the right one can only come following a diagnosis, which it feels society fights against. The amount of effort that I see clients go through to get the medication that helps them have the effort they need to get said medication is astonishing and concerning. I have seen people try to go the nonstimulant route after not being able to find stimulant medications, and some of them suffered the side effects enough that taking nothing was a better option for the time being.

Research by Taipale et al. (2024) discusses multifaceted benefits of medication for people with ADHD in the reduction of risk for psychiatric and nonpsychiatric hospitalizations. One such benefit is the reduction in suicidal behavior during periods of medicating as compared to periods with no intervention. Another is the decreased risk of workplace disability through nonstimulant medications [99]. At this point in our understanding of ADHD, we still struggle to identify a standard for treatment short of medication usage.

Corbisiero et al. (2018) discusses the use of what has been referred to as "minimal supportive therapy" in standard clinical management of an administered 30-minute meditation for the control group that was not found to be less beneficial than CBT in addition to this standard clinical management [100]. Science has seemed to struggle with the identification of treatment in the realm of ADHD outside the standardized use of medications despite backlash from politics and society. The argument seems to be based on what a person should be able to do versus what actually helps them, and this perspective is one of ableism.

ADHD medication is not the only thing affecting dopamine release in the brain. Forms of self-medicating can be problematic issues in impulse control pertaining to food, sex, and risky behaviors. Food can typically increase your dopamine by 10 times, sex by 100 times, and risky behavior likely falls above sex and below cocaine usage. So, there are behavioral solutions to meeting a person's needs, though these behaviors are often in addictive forms and maladaptive when depended upon for emotional need. However, this correlation gives hope to the idea that we can find behavioral intervention as described in the chapter on mindfulness.

Chapter 27

Government

The government tends to set standards and write laws regarding the treatment of ADHD from childhood through adulthood. The CDC recommends behavior management for children under six years old, medication and behavioral therapy for children over six, and anything and everything for adults who still meet the criteria for ADHD in adulthood, including medication, therapy, education, or some combination [101]. The FDA discusses approved treatments for children regarding medications and addresses the importance of treatment in relation to consequences of not being treated. For example, a child can be affected by falling behind in school, encountering difficulties in friendships, and having conflicts with parents if ADHD goes untreated [102].

These decisions seem to be based on the science and studies surrounding the safety and efficacy of treatments. The science is published and checked through peer review and likely is the most accurate information we have at this time. The government has also worked to promote the development of a video game [103] that can help with symptoms of ADHD. The research does not seem to be linked on that website currently, but I was able to find peer-reviewed articles that support its usage, such as the long-term benefits of the four-week intervention still being observed years later [104].

Another study looked at the efficacy of the video game treatment as compared to typical medication-based treatments for ADHD. The study found that medication is more effective than video game treatment, but both are still more effective than the control [105]. This does not include follow-up for long-term benefits years later, as was done in the previous study. And yet a third study looked at the usefulness of the game design type, specifically commercial versus "serious" video games. Commercial games already exist and were not designed for these purposes while serious games were developed and tested for ADHD. They found serious video games to have a better effect than commercial games due to the specific design for symptoms [106].

The government agencies dealing in science have found that both medication and treatment-based serious video games are part of the treatment process, with medication seeming to have a stronger effect, at least for the short term. Children are typically studied closely and taken care of through these forms of treatment.

So why is there such little research on the government's standardized practice or guidance for the treatment of ADHD in adults? The main treatment for adults following diagnosis seems to be medication and psychotherapy with little guidance toward the most effective process or treatment programming.

However, the prescription of medications has faced serious issues over the past several years due to changes within government oversight. The government agencies enacted changes in the quotas for production of medication for ADHD, which inhibited supply. They have since attempted to change these quotas while writing letters that also cast blame on everything other than their changes. For example, they noted a supply issue with one company while the shortage affected two separate stimulants made by many companies. The letter's first page contains both a non-apology and shifting responsibility with:

"The FDA and DEA do not manufacture drugs and cannot require a pharmaceutical company to make a drug, make more of a drug, or change the distribution of a drug. That said, we are working closely with numerous manufacturers, agencies, and others in the supply chain to understand, prevent, and reduce the impact of these shortages." [107]

The DEA and FDA then further state the companies had only produced 70% of what they were allotted and identify that as the reason for the shortage [107]. Counter to that argument:

"Makers of ADHD drugs say they do not have enough ingredients to make the drugs and need permission from the DEA to make more. The DEA is insisting that drugmakers have not met their quota for production and could make more of the drugs if they wanted." [107]

It appears everyone is pointing fingers at each other without a specific plan being promoted by the two entities engaged in production and enforcement. This is a failure *for* the people, not *by* the people.

To address the shortage, the DEA/FDA joint letter then focuses on alternative options that do not include stimulants, which is counter to the best practices suggested by research. They note their attempt to help people with ADHD:

"FDA has already taken steps to support the development of alternative treatment options. In 2020, for instance, FDA permitted marketing of a game-based digital therapeutic to improve attention function in children with ADHD." [107]

I am never a huge fan when in response to concern about not having something, the powers that be note how they have already helped. If the help worked, it would have been felt. This feels like gaslighting. The letter feels more like a dodge of responsibility to fix what was broken or enforce the needs of the people.

Heir of Narcissism

This issue of supply comes on top of requirements and costs of getting diagnosed and the wait time for a doctor or psychiatrist seemingly at a month minimum for treatment. People are paying an arm and a leg attempting to follow the prescribed path of bureaucracy and being stranded when their disability literally makes navigating these specific situations difficult. All the while, the brain of the person with ADHD is saying things like "maybe you're faking it" or "if you just buckled down and tried to focus more you wouldn't need the medication." These sentiments are then reinforced by the government's response shifting blame instead of providing noticeable support.

Why would the government be working like this? Not to sound like a conspiracy theorist, but it all started June 17th, 1971, when Richard Nixon gave a press conference, and the media coined the term the "war on drugs." A war we have never won. A war that has only ever become worse over time with the development of cheaper options of dangerous drugs that kill people. The war on drugs is more about stopping people from using rather than stopping people from dying.

This war was escalated by Reagan when he popularized the "Just Say No" campaign and the crackdown on crack. The pain that leads to drug addiction is like being held underwater as the urge to breathe becomes stronger and stronger every moment of every day. At some point, you are going to breathe. It just might not be air. Drugs are the poisonous gas in an air tank you randomly found that takes the desperation away for a time. It kills you slower, but you are not killed instantly by the root cause of said addiction. Only a fool would suggest removing the tank without replacing it with something else. An intelligent person would find a supply of air first, if possible, and if not, supply a safer alternative for the poison in the tank.

The war on drugs and "Just Say No" were never about drugs. They were about criminalizing pain so that we could lock away people the government harmed and society had failed. It was all part of the modern-day slave trade of inmate labor. Mandatory minimum sentencing makes no sense if the goal is to rehabilitate. It makes a lot of sense if you need cheap labor for a long time. Not everyone seems to know that the 13th Amendment did not abolish slavery. It legalized a specific kind of slavery:

"Neither slavery nor involuntary servitude, except as a punishment for crime whereof the party shall have been duly convicted, shall exist within the United States, or any place subject to their jurisdiction." [108]

The war on drugs was a pipeline from addiction to slavery. Ironic how earlier we discussed the definition of addict refers to a slave.

As I discussed earlier, addicts are often the unprotected children of our country who were harmed to such a degree that it seems only the drug can take away the pain as they get older and find a way to care for themselves maladaptively. It does not feel good to look at the pain that we might have once ignored, *so let us criminalize it and use these people for the benefit of society as slaves.* That is a disturbing thing to do to those we have failed to protect as a country.

But then again, the Supreme Court ruled that the government does not have a duty to protect in the *Town of Castle Rock, Colorado V. Gonzales* in 2005. Jessica Gonzales obtained a restraining order against the father of her three daughters. The girls were taken by their father in violation of this order, and Jessica called the Castle Rock Police Department. The police department told Jessica there was nothing they could do and for her to wait to see if their father brought them home later. She called and again was told to wait. After a time, she went to the police station to find nothing had been done to enforce the order. The husband showed up at the police station and opened fire. He was then killed in return fire from the police. The three girls were found dead in the back of his truck. The Supreme Court's decision was that due process does not grant the right to be protected by police in a 7-2 decision, even in the case of a violated restraining order [109].

We have not had a president in the White House that supports the proper treatment with stimulants for many, many years. Articles have since come out noting the improperly provided stimulants and sleep aids during the 2016 presidency [110]. The abuse of stimulants was going on while politicians were discussing the need for stronger punishments to substance users. During the 2020 administration, the president had a public struggle with his son whose drug of choice is a stimulant. It cannot be an accident that stimulant medications were disrupted during a time when a president's son was struggling with stimulant use disorders. Politics does not seem to want to support the proper treatment of the American people and often seems more likely to try and abuse power to practice beyond their scope of expertise without the support of the experts in the fields (see the *Chevron* case, which was overturned on July 8, 2024).

The psychiatric medications of stimulants, nonstimulants, and antidepressants all require a prescription. The government determines the ability of a person to write a prescription, and the practice of psychiatry is a dying field. It is being supplemented with general practitioners and nurse practitioners. Even with this supplementation, every facility I have worked at in my career had a deficit in the number of prescribers for mental health medications. Many referrals are for private pay and are unaffordable to most of the population. Will there ever be time for the government to develop a plan to institute the ability to add on education for prescribing rights? There was a bill in New Jersey that was aiming to affect this. I am not sure it ever worked out.

The government is also strongly affected by policies that wish to cause malicious suffering to its constituents. Someone once told me that a CEO does not care about productivity to make a few more million dollars a year. When you are that rich, it is the power and suffering you can inflict on others that brings joy.

I don't think this is completely inaccurate. The money made in backroom deals that harm so many people generate so little money compared to the suffering. One must assume suffering is the goal. A person cannot be sadistic in enjoying the implementation of pain while having access to empathy. A person cannot love without empathy.

There is a balance in humans that is directly correlated to my belief. There is a scale of love and hate in all of us. We cannot love someone while we hold hate for someone else. Love and hate cannot coexist in our hearts or minds. For the politicians that promote hate toward any specific people, I'm sorry you don't feel love. That is not an excuse to harm people beneath you. Grow up and get therapy. There is no reason to harm someone with less power than you, ever. Punching down is considered bad form, even in comedy where almost anything goes.

Chapter 28
Standard Direction

What is the standard direction for treatment of ADHD in the US? Well, stimulants seem to come out on top in many different studies. However, ADHD treatment is complex and seems to only be growing more complicated [111]. It seems there are many different forms of treatment being developed these days, creating difficulty in determining what is most efficacious. How do we determine the right forms of treatment for people with ADHD seeking help?

My therapist brain was raised in the controversial world of harm reduction. Perhaps in this book, where I do not focus on the cosigning of maladaptive coping skills, it might be more accepted. We need to understand what the problems beneath the symptoms of ADHD are to be able to truly treat them. However, there are signs of what we can treat with coping skills in the meantime while figuring out the source of the pain. People with ADHD have avoidant behaviors and similar ability to sit still and focus as a person who had been horribly traumatized. Whether we want to agree on that point is irrelevant, as the treatment would be the same either way.

In an introduction to trauma class during graduate school—actually, even earlier, such as in development or an introduction to psychology—we are taught about the need of a traumatized person. Maslow's hierarchy has a similar need to that of a traumatized person. Safety is the second-tier need, but food, water, air, and shelter are also what allow us to feel safe in the first place. The two first tiers of the hierarchy speak to us the need of a person before they can function with far less stress in society through love and belonging. We can likely assume that if the avoidant behaviors are to escape that space inside a person's head, the treatment must help make it safe.

I discuss all the time with clients that anger or even jealousy are secondary emotions. So is boredom. Have you ever sat in a room by yourself with nothing to do and not felt bored? Even once for 10 seconds? That tells us that boredom is triggered by something first. Boredom is the emotion of evasion. It tells us that wherever we are and whatever state we are in is not okay and something needs to change. It is our brain screaming to change the surroundings and the activity, because this one is not okay. So, my first goal in trauma or treatment with ADHD is to develop safety.

We need to develop safety in many different directions at once, as the call is coming from inside the house. The negative self-talk and cognitive distortions that bring shame and guilt onto the person need to be addressed quickly and with validation or CBT skills. The distress tolerance must be increased while being able to develop coping skills and not engaging in the urge to egress. Emotion regulation, from DBT, can be utilized to help a person manage the emotions whirling inside of them. Interpersonal effectiveness is also another valuable tool. We can finish the DBT toolbox with a little start of mindfulness in short bursts to maintain safety. I sometimes will warn the person about the difficulty in the triangle of trauma (discussed in Chapter 6) where their pain was so shameful, they had to handle it alone. I note how that should not be the case, and I am there to support them so they can ask for help when needed.

We build rapport and trust before discussing the roles in trauma or naming any specific person's words or actions.

Perhaps we look for the negative messages they get when guilt and shame are triggered. We discuss support systems and where to strengthen them. We discuss coping skills and what works for them. We provide psychoeducation and normalize typical responses to trauma or self-deprecating beliefs in people. We provide a space in which they can unravel everything safely in time and can return to "normal" between sessions.

If possible, we refer people we believe have ADHD to assessment for verification for pharmacological treatment. We refer them to a psychiatrist or psychiatric nurse practitioner, or, when that is impossible, a primary care physician. In a perfect world, this is part of an interdisciplinary team that all communicate. Though, that would be expensive and is less likely at a private practice level. A case manager, disability advocate, nurse navigator, and peer specialist would all be part of the dream team if it were feasible. At least they would be part of the beginning in developing that safe space through all aspects of the person's life.

That level of treatment is not realistic based on the current state of the medical system in our country outside of a community mental health center. A community mental health center that is already stretched thin on resources. Until that dream can be a reality, we must do our best to support people who need help and find safety. Honestly, the communities of neurodivergent people on the internet are not so bad in many cases. I have learned more about specific responses that bother me from ADHD in those communities than I did in graduate school or most books I have read on ADHD.

I do believe that family therapy would be part of a process to heal many of the maladaptive patterns in ADHD. As I have discussed throughout this book, the family system seems to play a role in the development of ADHD, at least through an epigenetic route. It would be unrealistic to expect change in the individual without change in the system. Perhaps that is also why stimulant treatments in children above the age of six seem effective. They struggle to change the system in which they have no power. However, the stimulants can clear the mind of a person with ADHD and create that safe space for them. Perhaps the standard treatment would be different based on age at the time of receiving it.

I believe the future of treatment for ADHD could be much more of a multidisciplinary approach that works with insurance and can reach all areas permitted by the person seeking support. Serious video games seem to show promise, though the price tag might be too high for some to afford. Perhaps other medical treatments will come along if society can hopefully change the stigma around the ADHD diagnosis and the prescription of stimulants. Maybe we will even find a definitive psychological treatment for the symptoms of ADHD. If we are dreaming big here, let's dream big. Hopefully, we understand the root cause of ADHD one day and find a treatment to manage the symptoms or reduce the maladaptive production of symptoms in the same way as when a traumatized person feels safe.

I don't know if there is a "cure" for ADHD or any other form of neurodivergence. I don't think that I would want to be cured even if there was. At this point in my life, my symptoms are more than manageable. They can be annoying at times, but I am relatively good on the day-to-day. I honestly would not even want to lose my superpowers. I would rather have a job or position in the world where they could be used for the benefit of others and my purpose would be fulfilled. It's wild how finding something that fulfills you can make so many of the symptoms seem to just disappear for a while.

I would love to find the answer to help so many people in the world with a similar issue. We do not have to go through life alone. We do not have to argue. If it works for you, take it. If it doesn't, leave it. I don't know if there can ever be a standardized care program. We don't have a standardized care model now across all the therapists in this country. Personalized medicine is on the rise. Perhaps ADHD treatment will have to follow that trend.

Perhaps, when society doesn't build us roads, we can trailblaze our own.

Afterword
A Call to Action

Trauma can be difficult to heal from in general. It is made even more difficult when we add in the complexities of complex trauma, a disorder in which a person learns to blame themselves for everything that goes wrong in their life and often blames luck for anything that goes right. We see the opposite in the type of person I believe causes this type of trauma. Narcissistic or even highly critical parenting seems to lead to these beliefs in complex trauma while the parent can blame the universe for their failures and accept all credit for successes. It doesn't seem fair. Healing complex trauma is difficult due to the nature of the survivor wanting to protect their parent or even close family member who might have as much as weekly access to the survivor.

It is hard to say that the perpetrators of the trauma in these processes are all narcissists as diagnosed by the DSM due to not having treated them, but the signs of narcissistic abuse are present in the survivors of this trauma. We can call them highly critical family members, but I have chosen to use the word narcissist for much of this book as it is the most recognizable term for what I am describing. I also specifically use this term due to the type of abuse that leads to complex trauma. I believe a form of CPTSD or a presentation of it is the culmination of symptoms we call ADHD. I believe the development of ADHD is both nature and nurture. The environment seems to play a strong role in the disorder's development through behavioral response and/or epigenetic expression.

There does not appear to be enough research yet to determine a strong correlation, let alone a causal relationship. However, I would make a call for more science to focus on this area of mental health for the development of a more standardized treatment and understanding in origin of the disorder ADHD. I believe we have used the genetic excuse for too many disorders in our history to make it okay not to know the origin. I do not believe that is a valid excuse as we begin to move more into the world of genetic sciences where we can change expression and develop gene therapies for issues that would have seemed impossible a decade ago.

The era of personalized medicine is beginning, and that starts with the understanding of the mechanisms by which our body and mind work. There needs to be more understanding of ADHD. If I am even slightly correct in my understanding of this disorder and its possible origin, we need to help the people who are suffering unnecessarily from trauma that was not their fault despite a belief it was. We need to learn how to strengthen resilience around the sense of self and help people develop coping skills to counter the abusive behaviors of emotionally immature parents, as Dr. Lindsay Gibson describes them.

Now is the time, due to the shift in generational beliefs. As Baby Boomers move out of the positions of power and Gen X/Millennials start to take the reins, it is time to start paying attention to the disorders that had been gaslit for so many years as just genetic or even fake. As the next generation of teachers, we need to recognize that laziness is simply a lack of motivation or fulfillment and that it is the early teachers' job especially to build this for our next generations. The bravery of Gen Z and their emotional awareness makes me want to see that health in all of us if possible.

There is time to heal many parent/child ruptures, as now seems to be the generation of forgiveness after accountability. Movies made today, such as Disney's *Encanto* [112] or *Turning Red* [113], have the theme of parents apologizing for the harm caused intentionally or unintentionally during childhood. I can't tell you how many times I have sat with an adult parent whose parents emotionally harmed them when they were children. These adult parents fear that their children will never forgive them for catching the intergenerational trauma too late. However, when asked if they would forgive their parents, requiring only an apology, they say of course, and some even tear up at the thought.

We are working with a pattern of abuse from early times in this country where war-torn men came home traumatized to raise a family in which those children grew up with their own wars and raised their own families while fighting the ghosts of the past on top of the ghosts of the past generations. Each generation got something wrong. The World Wars taught us peace was not guaranteed. The Great Depression taught us that resources, food, water, and shelter were not guaranteed. We were taught that our safety was never guaranteed. Baby Boomers and Gen X were able to mostly provide basic needs and in many cases safety. Millennials and Gen Z were able to strengthen the resolve of love and belonging, with Gen Z even going farther into self-esteem.

Every generation seems to try to heal some of the needs left unmet by the past generations while also falling short for the next generations of the new needs yet to be met. There also seems to be a phase in each generation of criticizing the next and past generations. I did this as a Millennial toward Millennials for years before accepting it. I then turned on Gen Z until I saw the emotional intelligence of the generation. Gen Z has started criticizing other generations in their turn at the wheel, and soon Gen Alpha will do the same to them.

Heir of Narcissism

We are remarkably similar despite the different histories. We carry the same trauma and can heal one another with validation and understanding. May the healing we have done and the wisdom we have found remove another spoke from the wheel for those who come next until its cycle can be broken.

References

Chapter 1

[1] McCarty CA, Lau AS, Valeri SM, Weisz JR. Parent-child interactions in relation to critical and emotionally overinvolved expressed emotion (EE): is EE a proxy for behavior? J Abnorm Child Psychol. 2004 Feb;32(1):83-93. doi: 10.1023/b:jacp.0000007582.61879.6f. PMID: 14998113; PMCID: PMC1352329.

[2] Rapp AM, Chavira DA, Sugar CA, Asarnow JR. Incorporating family factors into treatment planning for adolescent depression: Perceived parental criticism predicts longitudinal symptom trajectory in the Youth Partners in Care trial. J Affect Disord. 2021 Jan 1;278:46-53. doi: 10.1016/j.jad.2020.09.028. Epub 2020 Sep 11. PMID: 32949872; PMCID: PMC7704900.

[3] Young R, Lennie S, Minnis H. Children's perceptions of parental emotional neglect and control and psychopathology. J Child Psychol Psychiatry. 2011 Aug;52(8):889-97. doi: 10.1111/j.1469-7610.2011.02390.x. Epub 2011 Mar 25. PMID: 21438874; PMCID: PMC3170712.

[4] Gillihan, SJ. 16 signs of being raised by a highly critical parent. Psychology Today. 2022 Dec 8. https://www.psychologytoday.com/us/blog/think-act-be/202212/16-signs-of-being-raised-by-a-highly-critical-parent

Chapter 2

[5] Wulff AN, Thomas AK. The Dynamic and Fragile Nature of Eyewitness Memory Formation: Considering Stress and Attention. Front Psychol. 2021 Apr 13;12:666724. doi: 10.3389/fpsyg.2021.666724. PMID: 33927674; PMCID: PMC8076587.

[6] Yilmaz, AS. Eyewitness Memory: How Stress and Situational Factors Affect Eyewitness Recall (thesis). University of Oregon Scholars' Bank. December 2016. Retrieved January 6, 2025, from https://scholarsbank.uoregon.edu.

[7] Schwaba T, Bleidorn W, Hopwood CJ, Gebauer JE, Rentfrow PJ, Potter J, Gosling SD. The impact of childhood lead exposure on adult personality: Evidence from the United States, Europe, and a large-scale natural experiment. Proc Natl Acad Sci U S A. 2021 Jul 20;118(29):e2020104118. doi: 10.1073/pnas.2020104118. PMID: 34253605; PMCID: PMC8307752.

Chapter 3

[8] Wikimedia Foundation. (2023, December 17). *Cycle of abuse*. Wikipedia. https://en.wikipedia.org/wiki/Cycle_of_abuse

Chapter 4

[9] *Can you get brain damage from narcissistic abuse?*. Venture Academy. (2024, January 16). https://www.ventureacademy.ca/troubled-teen-blog/can-you-get-brain-damage-from-narcissistic-abuse/

[10] Gruner P, Pittenger C. Cognitive inflexibility in Obsessive-Compulsive Disorder. Neuroscience. 2017 Mar 14;345:243-255. doi: 10.1016/j.neuroscience.2016.07.030. Epub 2016 Aug 1. PMID: 27491478; PMCID: PMC5288350.

[11] Zhong W, Cristofori I, Bulbulia J, Krueger F, Grafman J. Biological and cognitive underpinnings of religious fundamentalism. Neuropsychologia. 2017 Jun;100:18-25. doi: 10.1016/j.neuropsychologia.2017.04.009. Epub 2017 Apr 6. PMID: 28392301; PMCID: PMC5500821.

[12] Tribby, A. (2022, November 8). *Cortisol and cognition: How the stress hormone affects the brain*. Aviv Clinics USA. https://aviv-clinics.com/blog/brain-health/how-cortisol-stress-hormone-affects-brain-health

[13] Ambardar, S. (n.d.). *15 Traits of Adult Children of Narcissists: How To Reclaim Your Happiness after Emotional Abuse*. The Happiness Psychiatrist®. https://www.happinesspsychiatrist.com/post/15-traits-adult-children-of-narcissists

[14] Saeed, K. (2017, October 20). *Long-term narcissistic abuse can cause brain damage*. Psych Central. https://psychcentral.com/blog/liberation/2017/10/long-term-narcissistic-abuse-can-cause-brain-damage#1

[15] Goleman, D. (2005). Emotional intelligence: Why it can matter more than IQ. Bantam Books.

[16] Herman, JL. (2023). *Truth and repair: How trauma survivors envision justice*. Basic Books, Hachette Book Group.

Chapter 5

[17] Fox Searchlight Pictures. (2010). *127 Hours*. United States.

[18] Skinner, BF. Superstition in the pigeon. J Exp Psychol. 1948 Apr;38(2):168-72. doi: 10.1037/h0055873. PMID: 18913665.

Chapter 6

[19] Robertson, M., Saidman, A., Holzman, E., Carlson, N., Stonington, J., Taylor, K., & Deutsch, P. (2024, March 22). The Darkest Secret. *Quiet on Set: The Dark Side of Kids TV*. episode, Investigation Discovery.

[20] Oxner, R. (2022, March 10). *Kids in foster care who'd been victims of sex trafficking endured fresh abuse at a state shelter, report says*. The Texas Tribune. https://www.texastribune.org/2022/03/10/texas-shelter-sex-trafficking-children/

[21] Former New Orleans Police Officer Sentenced for Sexually Assaulting a 15-Year-Old Girl. (2023, March 14). *U.S. Attorney's Office, Eastern District of Louisiana*. Retrieved January 19, 2025, from https://www.justice.gov/usao-edla/pr/former-new-orleans-police-officer-sentenced-sexually-assaulting-15-year-old-girl.

[22] Attorney General Shapiro Charges Western PA Priest with Sexual Abuse. (2017, July 24). *Pennsylvania Office of Attorney General*. Retrieved January 19, 2025, from https://www.attorneygeneral.gov/taking-action/attorney-general-shapiro-charges-western-pa-priest-with-sexual-abuse/.

Chapter 7

[23] American Psychiatric Association. (2013). *Diagnostic and statistical manual of mental disorders* (5th ed.). https://doi.org/10.1176/appi.books.9780890425596

[24] National Center for PTSD. (2013, June 6). *PTSD and DSM-5*. U.S. Department of Veteran's Affairs. https://www.ptsd.va.gov/professional/treat/essentials/dsm5_ptsd.asp#two

[25] Perl O, Duek O, Kulkarni KR, Gordon C, Krystal JH, Levy I, Harpaz-Rotem I, Schiller D. Neural patterns differentiate traumatic from sad autobiographical memories in PTSD. Nat Neurosci. 2023 Dec;26(12):2226-2236. doi: 10.1038/s41593-023-01483-5. Epub 2023 Nov 30. PMID: 38036701.

Chapter 9

[26] NHS. (2022, May 13). *Complex PTSD - Post-traumatic stress disorder.* NHS choices. https://www.nhs.uk/mental-health/conditions/post-traumatic-stress-disorder-ptsd/complex/

[27] The Foundation for Post-Traumatic Healing and Complex Trauma Research. (n.d.). *What is complex post-traumatic stress disorder?*. CPTSDfoundation.org. https://cptsdfoundation.org/what-is-complex-post-traumatic-stress-disorder-cptsd/

[28] Gooden, B. (n.d.). *#WhyIStayed links.* beverlygooden.com. https://www.beverlygooden.com/links

[29] Nolan, C. (Director). (2010). *Inception* [Film]. Warner Bros.

Chapter 10

[30] Liu Q, Liu Y, Leng X, Han J, Xia F, Chen H. Impact of Chronic Stress on Attention Control: Evidence from Behavioral and Event-Related Potential Analyses. Neurosci Bull. 2020 Nov;36(11):1395-1410. doi: 10.1007/s12264-020-00549-9. Epub 2020 Sep 15. PMID: 32929635; PMCID: PMC7674527.

[31] Yaribeygi H, Panahi Y, Sahraei H, Johnston TP, Sahebkar A. The impact of stress on body function: A review. EXCLI

J. 2017 Jul 21;16:1057-1072. doi: 10.17179/excli2017-480. PMID: 28900385; PMCID: PMC5579396.

[32] Schulz, M., & Waldinger, R. (2023, February 10). *An 85-year Harvard study found the no. 1 thing that makes us happy in life: It helps us "live longer."* CNBC. https://www.cnbc.com/2023/02/10/85-year-harvard-study-found-the-secret-to-a-long-happy-and-successful-life.html

Chapter 11

[33] Heartspeak Productions. (2009). *Brain Development & Addiction with Gabor Mate. YouTube.* Retrieved January 25, 2025, from https://www.youtube.com/watch?v=BpHiFqXCYKc.

[34] Groening, M., Cohen, D. X., & Vebber, D. (2003, July 23). Obsoletely Fabulous. *Futurama.* episode.

[35] Gmoney. (2008, April 1). *JFT April 1 - love and addiction - soberrecovery: Alcoholism drug addiction help and information.* SoberRecovery. https://www.soberrecovery.com/forums/narcotics-addiction-12-step-support/147267-jft-april-1-love-addiction.html

Chapter 12

[36] *Causes of PTSD: Childhood abuse.* PTSD UK. (n.d.). https://www.ptsduk.org/causes-of-ptsd-childhood-abuse/

[37] Young, A. (2019). The Place We Find Ourselves Podcast. episode.

[38] Spratt EG, Friedenberg SL, Swenson CC, Larosa A, De Bellis MD, Macias MM, Summer AP, Hulsey TC, Runyan DK, Brady KT. The Effects of Early Neglect on Cognitive,

Language, and Behavioral Functioning in Childhood. Psychology (Irvine). 2012 Feb 1;3(2):175-182. doi: 10.4236/psych.2012.32026. PMID: 23678396; PMCID: PMC3652241.

[39] Connor, T. (2017, February 14). *Recover Out Loud*. YouTube. https://www.youtube.com/watch?v=iAO5cBDvLlc

[40] Stern A, Agnew-Blais J, Danese A, Fisher HL, Jaffee SR, Matthews T, Polanczyk GV, Arseneault L. Associations between abuse/neglect and ADHD from childhood to young adulthood: A prospective nationally-representative twin study. Child Abuse Negl. 2018 Jul;81:274-285. doi: 10.1016/j.chiabu.2018.04.025. Epub 2018 May 15. PMID: 29775871; PMCID: PMC6013278.

[41] Capusan AJ, Kuja-Halkola R, Bendtsen P, Viding E, McCrory E, Marteinsdottir I, Larsson H. Childhood maltreatment and attention deficit hyperactivity disorder symptoms in adults: a large twin study. Psychol Med. 2016 Sep;46(12):2637-46. doi: 10.1017/S0033291716001021. Epub 2016 Jul 5. PMID: 27376862.

[42] Shafir, H. (2024, August 15). *ADHD & narcissism: Understanding the connection*. ChoosingTherapy.com. https://www.choosingtherapy.com/adhd-and-narcissism/

[43] Duarte M, Blay M, Hasler R, Pham E, Nicastro R, Jan M, Debbané M, Perroud N. Adult ADHD and pathological narcissism: A retrospective-analysis. J Psychiatr Res. 2024 Jun;174:245-253. doi: 10.1016/j.jpsychires.2024.04.032. Epub 2024 Apr 21. PMID: 38670059.

Chapter 13

[44] Maté, G., & Polish, J. (2018, February 20). *Dr. Gabor Maté In the Realm of Hungry Ghosts.* YouTube. https://www.youtube.com/watch?v=VvQYwOlx0HY

[45] Zulauf CA, Sprich SE, Safren SA, Wilens TE. The complicated relationship between attention deficit/hyperactivity disorder and substance use disorders. Curr Psychiatry Rep. 2014 Mar;16(3):436. doi: 10.1007/s11920-013-0436-6. PMID: 24526271; PMCID: PMC4414493.

[46] Humphreys KL, Eng T, Lee SS. Stimulant medication and substance use outcomes: a meta-analysis. JAMA Psychiatry. 2013 Jul;70(7):740-9. doi: 10.1001/jamapsychiatry.2013.1273. PMID: 23754458; PMCID: PMC6688478.

[33] Heartspeak Productions. (2009). *Brain Development & Addiction with Gabor Mate. YouTube.* Retrieved January 25, 2025, from https://www.youtube.com/watch?v=BpHiFqXCYKc.

[47] World Health Organization(WHO). (1993). *The ICD-10 classification of mental and behavioural disorders* (Version:2016). World Health Organization. https://icd.who.int/browse10/2016/en#/F60-F69

[48] Nicol AU, Morton AJ. Characteristic patterns of EEG oscillations in sheep (Ovis aries) induced by ketamine may explain the psychotropic effects seen in humans. Sci Rep. 2020 Jun 11;10(1):9440. doi: 10.1038/s41598-020-66023-8. PMID: 32528071; PMCID: PMC7289807.

Chapter 14

[49] Luderer M, Ramos Quiroga JA, Faraone SV, Zhang James Y, Reif A. Alcohol use disorders and ADHD. Neurosci Biobehav Rev. 2021 Sep;128:648-660. doi: 10.1016/j.neubiorev.2021.07.010. Epub 2021 Jul 12. Erratum in: Neurosci Biobehav Rev. 2021 Nov;130:227. doi: 10.1016/j.neubiorev.2021.08.026. PMID: 34265320.

[50] Appleman, K. (n.d.). *U.S. alcohol issue: A neglected deadly epidemic.* Caron Treatment Centers. https://www.caron.org/blog/the-american-alcohol-problem

[51] U.S. Department of Health and Human Services. (n.d.). *Attention-deficit/hyperactivity disorder (ADHD).* National Institute of Mental Health. https://www.nimh.nih.gov/health/statistics/attention-deficit-hyperactivity-disorder-adhd

[52] *Alcohol and ADHD.* Alcohol Help. (2024, November 7). https://www.alcoholhelp.com/resources/dual-diagnosis/alcohol-and-adhd/

[53] *Proprioception explained.* Brain Balance Achievement Centers. (n.d.). https://www.brainbalancecenters.com/blog/proprioception-explained

[54] Barkley RA, Fischer M. Hyperactive Child Syndrome and Estimated Life Expectancy at Young Adult Follow-Up: The Role of ADHD Persistence and Other Potential Predictors. J Atten Disord. 2019 Jul;23(9):907-923. doi: 10.1177/1087054718816164. Epub 2018 Dec 10. PMID: 30526189.

Chapter 15

[55] Dhamija D, Bello AO, Khan AA, Gutlapalli SD, Sohail M, Patel PA, Midha S, Shukla S, Mohammed L. Evaluation of Efficacy of Cannabis Use in Patients With Attention Deficit Hyperactivity Disorder: A Systematic Review. Cureus. 2023 Jun 26;15(6):e40969. doi: 10.7759/cureus.40969. PMID: 37503496; PMCID: PMC10370827.

[56] Teplin, D. (2019, June). *ADHD & recreational marijuana: What's the attraction?* Children and Adults with Attention-Deficit/Hyperactivity Disorder (CHADD). https://chadd.org/attention-article/adhd-recreational-marijuana/

Chapter 16

[57] Palmiter RD. Dopamine signaling in the dorsal striatum is essential for motivated behaviors: lessons from dopamine-deficient mice. Ann N Y Acad Sci. 2008;1129:35-46. doi: 10.1196/annals.1417.003. PMID: 18591467; PMCID: PMC2720267.

[58] Daubner SC, Le T, Wang S. Tyrosine hydroxylase and regulation of dopamine synthesis. Arch Biochem Biophys. 2011 Apr 1;508(1):1-12. doi: 10.1016/j.abb.2010.12.017. Epub 2010 Dec 19. PMID: 21176768; PMCID: PMC3065393.

[59] WebMD. (2023, May 15). *Stimulant medications for ADHD treatment: Types, side effects, and more.* WebMD. https://www.webmd.com/add-adhd/adhd-stimulant-therapy

[60] Benson K, Woodlief DT, Flory K, Siceloff ER, Coleman K, Lamont A. Is ADHD, independent of ODD, associated with whether and why college students misuse stimulant

medication? Exp Clin Psychopharmacol. 2018 Oct;26(5):476-487. doi: 10.1037/pha0000202. Epub 2018 Jun 28. PMID: 29952616.

[33] Heartspeak Productions. (2009). *Brain Development & Addiction with Gabor Mate. YouTube.* Retrieved January 25, 2025, from https://www.youtube.com/watch?v=BpHiFqXCYKc.

Chapter 17

[61] Sussex Publishers. (n.d.). *Nature vs. nurture.* Psychology Today. https://www.psychologytoday.com/us/basics/nature-vs-nurture

[62] McLeod, S. (2023, June 15). *Harry Harlow Monkey experiments: Cloth mother vs wire mother.* Simply Psychology. https://www.simplypsychology.org/harlow-monkey.html

[63] *Alcoholics anonymous big book* (4th ed.). (2002). Alcoholics Anonymous World Services.

[64] du Plessis, S. (2023, April 9). *Victor of Aveyron - the story of a feral child.* Edublox Online Tutor. https://www.edubloxtutor.com/victor-feral-child/

[65] Brogaard, B. (2017, July 10). *The feral child nicknamed Genie.* Psychology Today. https://www.psychologytoday.com/us/blog/the-superhuman-mind/201707/the-feral-child-nicknamed-genie

[66] *Opportunity atlas shows the effect of childhood ZIP codes on adult success.* Local Initiatives Support Corporation. (n.d.). https://www.lisc.org/our-resources/resource/opportunity-atlas-shows-effect-childhood-zip-codes-adult-success/

[67] Dekkers TJ, Hornstra R, van den Hoofdakker BJ, de Jong SRC, Schaaf JV, Bosmans G, van der Oord S. Attachment Representations in Children with and without Attention-Deficit/Hyperactivity Disorder (ADHD). Brain Sci. 2021 Nov 16;11(11):1516. doi: 10.3390/brainsci11111516. PMID: 34827515; PMCID: PMC8615467.

Chapter 18

[68] Longden, E. (2013, February). *The voices in my head.* TED. https://www.ted.com/talks/eleanor_longden_the_voices_in_my_head

[69] Plomin R, DeFries JC, Knopik VS, Neiderhiser JM. Top 10 Replicated Findings From Behavioral Genetics. Perspect Psychol Sci. 2016 Jan;11(1):3-23. doi: 10.1177/1745691615617439. PMID: 26817721; PMCID: PMC4739500.

[70] *Karl Lashley*. Harvard University Department of Psychology. (n.d.). https://psychology.fas.harvard.edu/people/karl-lashley

[71] Youssef NA, Lockwood L, Su S, Hao G, Rutten BPF. The Effects of Trauma, with or without PTSD, on the Transgenerational DNA Methylation Alterations in Human Offsprings. Brain Sci. 2018 May 8;8(5):83. doi: 10.3390/brainsci8050083. PMID: 29738444; PMCID: PMC5977074.

[72] Jin B, Li Y, Robertson KD. DNA methylation: superior or subordinate in the epigenetic hierarchy? Genes Cancer. 2011 Jun;2(6):607-17. doi: 10.1177/1947601910393957. PMID: 21941617; PMCID: PMC3174260.

Chapter 19

[73] Moosavi A, Motevalizadeh Ardekani A. Role of Epigenetics in Biology and Human Diseases. Iran Biomed J. 2016 Nov;20(5):246-58. doi: 10.22045/ibj.2016.01. Epub 2016 Jul 5. PMID: 27377127; PMCID: PMC5075137.

[74] *Health impacts of intergenerational trauma.* Johns Hopkins Center for Indigenous Health. (2021, October 26). https://cih.jhu.edu/what-we-do/resources/health-impacts-of-intergenerational-trauma/

[75] Winfield A, Sugar C, Fenesi B. The impact of the COVID-19 pandemic on the mental health of families dealing with attention-deficit hyperactivity disorder. PLoS One. 2023 Mar 16;18(3):e0283227. doi: 10.1371/journal.pone.0283227. PMID: 36928863; PMCID: PMC10019744.

Chapter 20

[76] Leithead, K. (2025, January 30). *False reports – percentage.* End Violence Against Women International. https://evawintl.org/best_practice_faqs/false-reports-percentage/

[77] Hagborg JM, Kalin T, Gerdner A. The Childhood Trauma Questionnaire-Short Form (CTQ-SF) used with adolescents - methodological report from clinical and community samples. J Child Adolesc Trauma. 2022 Mar 30;15(4):1199-1213. doi: 10.1007/s40653-022-00443-8. PMID: 36439669; PMCID: PMC9684390.

[78] Troisi G. Measuring Intimate Partner Violence and Traumatic Affect: Development of VITA, an Italian Scale. Front Psychol. 2018 Jul 26;9:1282. doi: 10.3389/fpsyg.2018.01282. PMID: 30093875; PMCID: PMC6070688.

Chapter 21

[79] *Ram Dass – here and now podcast.* Be Here Now Network. (n.d.). https://beherenownetwork.com/category/ram-dass/

[80] Maidenberg, M. P. (2022, March 3). *The Healing Power of Radical Acceptance.* Psychology Today. https://www.psychologytoday.com/us/blog/being-your-best-self/202203/the-healing-power-of-radical-acceptance

[81] *The original serenity prayer by Reinhold Niebuhr.* Proactive 12 Steps. (2022, May 27). https://proactive12steps.com/serenity-prayer/

[82] Kabat-Zinn, J. (2011, April 13). *The Healing Power of Mindfulness.* YouTube. https://www.youtube.com/watch?v=_If4a-gHg_I

[83] Niazi AK, Niazi SK. Mindfulness-based stress reduction: a non-pharmacological approach for chronic illnesses. N Am J Med Sci. 2011 Jan;3(1):20-3. doi: 10.4297/najms.2011.320. PMID: 22540058; PMCID: PMC3336928.

[84] Alda M, Puebla-Guedea M, Rodero B, Demarzo M, Montero-Marin J, Roca M, Garcia-Campayo J. Zen meditation, Length of Telomeres, and the Role of Experiential Avoidance and Compassion. Mindfulness (N Y). 2016;7:651-659. doi: 10.1007/s12671-016-0500-5. Epub 2016 Feb 22. PMID: 27217844; PMCID: PMC4859856.

[32] Schulz, M., & Waldinger, R. (2023, February 10). *An 85-year Harvard study found the no. 1 thing that makes us happy in life: It helps us "live longer."* CNBC. https://www.cnbc.com/2023/02/10/85-year-harvard-study-found-the-secret-to-a-long-happy-and-successful-life.html

[85] Kim Y, Khil J, Wangmo-Seo, Keum N. The Effects of Mindfulness and Buddhist Meditation Coaching on Mental Health Outcomes in College Students. Evid Based Complement Alternat Med. 2022 Nov 24;2022:8178930. doi: 10.1155/2022/8178930. PMID: 36467551; PMCID: PMC9715338.

Chapter 22

[86] Overbay, T. [@virtualcouch]. (n.d.). [TikTok profile]. TikTok. Retrieved on February 10, 2025, from https://www.tiktok.com/@virtualcouch

[87] Overbay, T. [@virtualcouch]. (2023, March 17). Today, I'd like to introduce you to my popcorn moments. This is the origin story in regards to these special [Video] TikTok. https://www.tiktok.com/@virtualcouch/video/7211579207330172202

Chapter 23

[88] Orenstein GA, Lewis L. Erikson's Stages of Psychosocial Development. 2022 Nov 7. In: StatPearls [Internet]. Treasure Island (FL): StatPearls Publishing; 2025 Jan–. PMID: 32310556.

[89] Allé MC, Berntsen D. Self-isolation, psychotic symptoms and cognitive problems during the COVID-19 worldwide outbreak. Psychiatry Res. 2021 Aug;302:114015. doi: 10.1016/j.psychres.2021.114015. Epub 2021 May 19. PMID: 34062477; PMCID: PMC8131183.

[90] Leach J. Psychological factors in exceptional, extreme and torturous environments. Extrem Physiol Med. 2016 Jun 1;5:7. doi: 10.1186/s13728-016-0048-y. PMID: 27257476; PMCID: PMC4890253.

Chapter 24

[91] Schwaba T, Bleidorn W, Hopwood CJ, Gebauer JE, Rentfrow PJ, Potter J, Gosling SD. The impact of childhood lead exposure on adult personality: Evidence from the United States, Europe, and a large-scale natural experiment. Proc Natl Acad Sci U S A. 2021 Jul 20;118(29):e2020104118. doi: 10.1073/pnas.2020104118. PMID: 34253605; PMCID: PMC8307752.

Chapter 25

[92] Abdelnour E, Jansen MO, Gold JA. ADHD Diagnostic Trends: Increased Recognition or Overdiagnosis? Mo Med. 2022 Sep-Oct;119(5):467-473. PMID: 36337990; PMCID: PMC9616454.

[93] *FAQ's*. Council on Compulsive Gambling of PA. (n.d.). https://www.pacouncil.com/problem-gambling/faqs/#12

[94] Yale Medicine. (n.d.). *Gambling disorder*. Yale Medicine. https://www.yalemedicine.org/conditions/gambling-disorder

Chapter 26

[95] de Jong M, Wynchank DSMR, van Andel E, Beekman ATF, Kooij JJS. Female-specific pharmacotherapy in ADHD: premenstrual adjustment of psychostimulant dosage. Front Psychiatry. 2023 Dec 13;14:1306194. doi: 10.3389/fpsyt.2023.1306194. PMID: 38152361; PMCID: PMC10751335.

[96] FDA. (n.d.). *FDA history milestones*. U.S. Food and Drug Administration. https://www.fda.gov/about-fda/fda-history/milestones-us-food-and-drug-law

[97] Thompson, J. (2023, August 22). *No one studied menstrual product absorbency realistically until now*. Scientific American. https://www.scientificamerican.com/article/no-one-studied-menstrual-product-absorbency-realistically-until-now/

[98] Shearston JA, Upson K, Gordon M, Do V, Balac O, Nguyen K, Yan B, Kioumourtzoglou MA, Schilling K. Tampons as a source of exposure to metal(loid)s. Environ Int. 2024 Aug;190:108849. doi: 10.1016/j.envint.2024.108849. Epub 2024 Jun 22. PMID: 38963987.

[99] Taipale H, Bergström J, Gèmes K, Tanskanen A, Ekselius L, Mittendorfer-Rutz E, Helgesson M. Attention-Deficit/Hyperactivity Disorder Medications and Work Disability and Mental Health Outcomes. JAMA Netw Open. 2024 Mar 4;7(3):e242859. doi: 10.1001/jamanetworkopen.2024.2859. PMID: 38506810; PMCID: PMC10955386.

[100] Corbisiero S, Bitto H, Newark P, Abt-Mörstedt B, Elsässer M, Buchli-Kammermann J, Künne S, Nyberg E, Hofecker-Fallahpour M, Stieglitz RD. A Comparison of Cognitive-Behavioral Therapy and Pharmacotherapy vs. Pharmacotherapy Alone in Adults With Attention-Deficit/Hyperactivity Disorder (ADHD)-A Randomized Controlled Trial. Front Psychiatry. 2018 Nov 16;9:571. doi: 10.3389/fpsyt.2018.00571. PMID: 30505283; PMCID: PMC6250816.

Chapter 27

[101] Centers for Disease Control and Prevention. (2024, May 16). *Treatment of ADHD*. Centers for Disease Control and Prevention. https://www.cdc.gov/adhd/treatment/

[102] FDA. (2023, August 28). *Treating and Dealing with ADHD.* U.S. Food and Drug Administration. https://www.fda.gov/consumers/consumer-updates/treating-and-dealing-adhd

[103] *Efficacy - endeavorrx®.* EndeavorRx. (2023, October 25). https://www.hcpendeavorrx.com/efficacy/

[104] Jurigova BG, Gerdes MR, Anguera JA, Marco EJ. Sustained benefits of cognitive training in children with inattention, three-year follow-up. PLoS One. 2021 Feb 4;16(2):e0246449. doi: 10.1371/journal.pone.0246449. PMID: 33539468; PMCID: PMC7861383.

[105] Oh S, Choi J, Han DH, Kim E. Effects of game-based digital therapeutics on attention deficit hyperactivity disorder in children and adolescents as assessed by parents or teachers: a systematic review and meta-analysis. Eur Child Adolesc Psychiatry. 2024 Feb;33(2):481-493. doi: 10.1007/s00787-023-02174-z. Epub 2023 Mar 2. PMID: 36862162.

[106] Sújar A, Martín-Moratinos M, Rodrigo-Yanguas M, Bella-Fernández M, González-Tardón C, Delgado-Gómez D, Blasco-Fontecilla H. Developing Serious Video Games to Treat Attention Deficit Hyperactivity Disorder: Tutorial Guide. JMIR Serious Games. 2022 Aug 1;10(3):e33884. doi: 10.2196/33884. PMID: 35916694; PMCID: PMC9379781.

[107] Joint DEA FDA Letter. (2023, August 1). *U.S. Food and Drug Administration.* Retrieved February 10, 2025, from https://www.fda.gov/media/170736/download.

[108] U.S. Const. amend. XIII. Retrieved from https://www.archives.gov/milestone-documents/13th-amendment

[109] Teitelbaum J, Coogan VN, Rosenbaum S. Town of Castle Rock, Colorado v Gonzales: implications for public health policy and practice. Public Health Rep. 2006 May-Jun;121(3):337-9. doi: 10.1177/003335490612100318. PMID: 16640159; PMCID: PMC1525280.

[110] Aboulenein, A. (2024, January 28). *Trump White House Pharmacy improperly provided drugs and misused funds, Pentagon report says*. Reuters. https://www.reuters.com/world/us/trump-white-house-pharmacy-improperly-provided-drugs-misused-funds-pentagon-2024-01-28/

Chapter 28

[111] Nazarova VA, Sokolov AV, Chubarev VN, Tarasov VV, Schiöth HB. Treatment of ADHD: Drugs, psychological therapies, devices, complementary and alternative methods as well as the trends in clinical trials. Front Pharmacol. 2022 Nov 17;13:1066988. doi: 10.3389/fphar.2022.1066988. PMID: 36467081; PMCID: PMC9713849.

Afterward

[112] Bush, J., & Howard, B. (Directors). (2021). *Encanto* [Film]. Walt Disney Pictures; Walt Disney Animation Studios.

[113] Shi, D. (Director). (2022). *Turning Red* [Film]. Walt Disney Pictures; Walt Disney Animation Studios.

Additional Reading

Response from manufacturers regarding ADHD medication shortage: Lovelace, B. (2024, February 6). *"I'm fed up": Frustrations grow as ADHD drug shortage continues.* NBCNews.com. https://www.nbcnews.com/health/health-news/adhd-drug-shortage-adderall-ritalin-focalin-vyvanse-rcna137356

Neurodivergence and the cerebellum: Stoodley CJ. The Cerebellum and Neurodevelopmental Disorders. Cerebellum. 2016 Feb;15(1):34-37. doi: 10.1007/s12311-015-0715-3. PMID: 26298473; PMCID: PMC4811332.

DNA variants and risk genes for ADHD: Olfson E, Farhat LC, Liu W, Vitulano LA, Zai G, Lima MO, Parent J, Polanczyk GV, Cappi C, Kennedy JL, Fernandez TV. Rare de novo damaging DNA variants are enriched in attention-deficit/hyperactivity disorder and implicate risk genes. Nat Commun. 2024 Jul 12;15(1):5870. doi: 10.1038/s41467-024-50247-7. PMID: 38997333; PMCID: PMC11245598.

Emotional dysregulation in ADHD: Hou, W., Sahakian, B.J., Langley, C. *et al.* Emotion dysregulation and right pars orbitalis constitute a neuropsychological pathway to attention deficit hyperactivity disorder. *Nat. Mental Health* **2**, 840–852 (2024). https://doi.org/10.1038/s44220-024-00251-z.

Glossary

ADHD: Attention Deficit/Hyperactivity Disorder is a disorder often found somewhere between impulse control and cognitive processing disorders where it properly fits closer to an emotion regulation disorder.

Anxious-ambivalent attachment: An insecure attachment style that is characterized by an emotionally overbearing nature due to anxiety or complete apathy toward a relationship that has been harmful.

Aphantasia: The neurological inability to visualize within the mind to varying degrees.

Autonomy: The ability to self-govern, make decisions, and act for oneself at one's own direction.

Bottom-up thinking: A type of thinking often characterizing neurodivergent thought that starts from detailed information and builds to larger concepts.

Catecholamines: A class of molecules that function throughout the body as either neurotransmitters or hormones. Dopamine, norepinephrine (noradrenaline), and epinephrine (adrenaline) are all catecholamines.

CBT: Cognitive Behavioral Therapy is one of the most studied forms of treatment.

Countertransference: The response, often of a therapist, to the projected emotion of others onto them.

CPTSD: Complex Posttraumatic Stress Disorder is a form of PTSD that is made complex by the nature of having to defend those who have caused harm.

Cycle of abuse: A cycle that is common to nearly all systems of abuse.

Dark triad: Three major areas of narcissism that show how the maladaptive traits are presenting.

DARVO: Deny, Attack, Reverse Victim and Offender is the pattern many abusers will use to victimize themselves while claiming the person they have harmed is actually harming them.

DBT: Dialectical Behavioral Therapy was developed by Marsha Linehan to treat Borderline Personality Disorder and is also affective for the treatment of trauma.

Depersonalization: A form of dissociation that makes it seem as if you are not yourself.

Derealization: A form of dissociation that makes the world feel as if it is not real.

Dismissive-avoidant attachment: A form of insecure attachment that is often apathetic to the idea of connection in part due to the pain of disconnection.

Dissociation: Feeling disconnected from the world in what can feel like being on autopilot.

Distress tolerance: The ability to experience discomfort of distressing emotions for a time.

DOPA: L-DOPA is a precursor molecule in the formation of catecholamines.

Downers: Substances that have a depressing or sedative-like effect on a person.

DSM: The Diagnostic and Statistical Manual or the American catalog of psychological disorders.

Egress: The act of leaving a space or an exit.

Emergent need: A need that has reached such a level that it can no longer wait to be met.

Emotional equity: The value of acts done in the building of debt through emotional guilt.

Emotional incest: An improper emotional relationship from parent to child where the child is given the emotional responsibilities of a spouse to said parent.

Existentialism-based therapy: A type of therapy that questions the purpose of existence and notes that anxiety derives from the overwhelming choice.

Explicit/recall memory: The type of memory that is often video or pictures in our heads.

Fearful-avoidant attachment: An insecure attachment style derived from fear of a caretaker.

Gestalt therapy: A type of therapy developed by German psychologists during the mid-1900s that focuses on the perception of the mind and focuses on the here and now unless the past is relevant.

Golden child: The child that is given praise for doing well and operates in a form of golden handcuffs in which their value is derived from success alone.

Highly critical parent: A parent who is critical toward the world or a child to such a degree that it is harmful to a child's psyche.

Historical trauma: Trauma that has affected portions of the population alive at the time of said trauma (such as 9/11).

ICD 10: The international version of the DSM.

Implicit memory: A form of memory that is stored in the body and often presents as the physical sensation of emotional response.

Intergenerational trauma: Trauma that is handed down through generations through genetics and/or behavioral traits.

Interoception: The ability to sense and perceive the body's internal stimuli/state.

Learned helplessness: A reaction that develops when no right choice is available to avoid pain. Often the individual will lay down and stop trying to change their environment or end suffering.

Limbic system: The emotional nervous system and portion of the brain that regulates emotion, memory, and behavior.

Love bombing: The act of overly giving to another person early in the relationship to generate high levels of emotional equity before the value of said actions depreciates.

Maladaptive coping strategies: Any coping skill that is harmful to the person using it.

MBSR: Mindfulness Based Stress Reduction is the CBT of mindfulness and developed by Dr. Jon Kabat Zinn.

Mirroring: Responding to a child in a similar level of emotion, often excitement.

Narcissistic abuse cycle: A cycle of abuse like the cycle of abuse with an extra step of abandonment.

NCPE: Non-Consensual Performative Emotion is what others expect of you without concern of your desire to provide this emotion (men telling women to smile more).

NDRI: Norepinephrine–dopamine reuptake inhibitor, a medication that works on the neurotransmitters norepinephrine and dopamine to reduce the reuptake action of the brain. This is used as an antidepressant and to assist in medicating ADHD.

Negative: Used in psychology to mean something is removed rather than something is bad.

Nonduality: A belief that everything is one and there is no this and that. Rather the belief that this and that are two sides of the same coin.

NPD: Narcissistic Personality Disorder is the official diagnosis listed in the DSM.

OCD: Obsessive-Compulsive Disorder is a disorder defined by preoccupation over irresistible urges to perform rituals that feel as though they can reduce anxiety through magical means.

Positive: The addition to anything under the psychological definition.

Positive psychology: A form of psychology that focuses on the happy or additive properties of psychology with a focus on making life better.

Proprioception: The sense of the brain of where parts of the body exist in space at any given time.

Protective factors: Aspects of a person's belief system or support system that would prevent them from engaging in harmful or maladaptive behaviors.

PTSD: Posttraumatic Stress Disorder is a disorder developed in response to extreme levels of stress either in a single instance or many traumas over time.

Punishment: Infliction of a penalty in response to an action.

Reinforcement: Encouragement of a behavior through action following the desired result to further entrench a behavior in response to a triggering action.

Rejection Sensitive Dysphoria: Extreme emotional pain in response to rejection or perceived rejection.

Scapegoat: The person who responsibility is applied to relieve others of the burden of said responsibility.

Self-efficacy: A person's belief in their ability to achieve any given action.

Self-esteem: A person's positive or negative opinion of themselves.

Sense of self: A person's understanding of who they are as a person.

SLAPP: Lawsuits that are used by powerful people to silence others through prolonged litigation.

Sleep hygiene: Sleep behaviors that are used to maintain health relating to sleep and wakefulness.

SNRI: Serotonin–norepinephrine reuptake inhibitors work to give the brain more time to use the neurotransmitters in the name. This allows the brain to use these chemicals and creates a deficit that the brain will learn to budget for over the course of the 4-8 weeks it takes these medications to work.

SSRI: Selective serotonin reuptake inhibitors work to give the brain more time to use the neurotransmitters in the name. This allows the brain to use these chemicals and creates a deficit that the brain will learn to budget for over the course of the 4-8 weeks it takes these medications to work.

Stimulants: Medications that are known as uppers or make a person feel as though they have more energy.

Strength-based model: A model of psychotherapy that focuses on building the strength of a person so they will have the confidence to address their struggles.

Synapse: The place where neurons meet and communicate with each other through neurotransmitters.

Top-down thinking: Being able to take past knowledge to predict and apply to new situations.

Transference: The projection of emotions from past experience onto a current experience that may or may not have anything to do with said past experience.

Triangle of trauma: A relationship dynamic that typically involves at least three people including the perpetrator, victim, and unhelping bystander. This dynamic is often part of what makes trauma traumatic.

About the Author

Michael Drag is a Licensed Professional Counselor in the state of Pennsylvania and has been practicing since 2014. He was called to start his career in community mental health treating co-occurring disorders. He then practiced in a drug and alcohol rehab setting while entering the world of private practice. He specializes in trauma, which has led him to practice in addiction, neurodivergence, and adult survivors of childhood trauma in individual and group settings. After being diagnosed with ADHD as an adult, he has worked to increase understanding of this often-neglected area of treatment. He also believes his call to trauma was no accident. You can find him online at www.spacebetweenthewords.com.

Acknowledgments

I want to first thank Dr. Loren Logsdon without whom I would never have seen the potential to even graduate college. He saw something in me that it felt no one else, including myself, could see. May he rest in peace.

I also want to thank my ever-patient life partner who helped me to complete this book in spite of my ADHD wanting to wander around while we attempted to edit the final draft. Her encouragement gave me the confidence to finally sit down and write this book, which pales in comparison to her current catalog of more than 25 stories.

I finally want to acknowledge my family and the tolerance to be able to explore aspects of early life that might not have been exactly perfect. It is only through the openness of this exploration that I was able to understand myself within the context of this life.

www.ingramcontent.com/pod-product-compliance
Lightning Source LLC
Chambersburg PA
CBHW070141100426
42743CB00013B/2781